VINTAGE
GREENING THE EARTH

K. Satchidanandan is a bilingual poet, critic, playwright, editor, fiction writer and travel writer. He has worked as the editor of *Indian Literature* bimonthly and *Beyond Borders*, a South Asian Association for Regional Cooperation literature quarterly. He has thirty-two collections of poetry in the Malayalam and thirty-nine collections in the Arabic, Irish, French, German, Italian, Spanish, Chinese and Japanese besides all major Indian languages. He has won sixty-four literary awards, including the National Academy Award, Poet Laureate Award from the Tata Literature Festival, Bombay, Kanhaiyalal Sethia Memorial Poetry Award from the Jaipur Literature Festival and five awards in five genres from the Kerala Sahitya Akademi, of which he is currently the president and a fellow.

Nishi Chawla is a noted Asian-American poet and playwright. She has published nine plays, two novels and seven collections of poetry. She has also written and directed three award-winning feature films. She is presently making a movie on Gandhi, Martin Luther King, Jr and Thoreau. Nishi Chawla holds a doctorate in English from George Washington University, Washington, DC, and did her post-doctorate from Johns Hopkins University, USA. She has taught English Literature for forty years.

T0205219

Celebrating 35 Years of
Penguin Random House India

ALSO BY THE EDITORS

Singing in the Dark: A Global Anthology of Poetry Under Lockdown
(edited by K. Satchidanandan, Nishi Chawla)
Words Matter: Writings Against Silence
(edited by K. Satchidanandan)

greening the earth
a global anthology of poetry

K. Satchidanandan
& Nishi Chawla

VINTAGE
An imprint of Penguin Random House

VINTAGE

USA | Canada | UK | Ireland | Australia
New Zealand | India | South Africa | China

Vintage is part of the Penguin Random House group of companies
whose addresses can be found at global.penguinrandomhouse.com

Published by Penguin Random House India Pvt. Ltd
4th Floor, Capital Tower 1, MG Road,
Gurugram 122 002, Haryana, India

First published in Vintage by Penguin Random House India in 2023

ISBN 9780143463214

Typeset in Adobe Caslon Pro by Manipal Technologies Limited, Manipal

www.penguin.co.in

Preface

Our human environment has become the most crucial question that concerns the survival of the human species and our planet. It is not surprising that some of the hottest battles of our time are being fought around ecological issues, especially in the context of the aggressive developmental policies pursued by neo-liberal and often pro-imperialistic regimes across the globe. Global warming, ozone layer damage, fatal radiations, soil erosion, forest fires, industrial pollution, the drying up and depletion of rivers, floods and avalanches, irrational changes in weather patterns, the exhaustion of non-renewable resources due to the use of unsustainable developmental strategies (rationalized by what Ivan Illich termed 'industrial ideology'), social entropy and genetic manipulation that cut across national boundaries—these are driving issues that trigger immediate and intense reactions. Not only is the future of the human species at stake, but animals and plants are also facing extinction due to environmental damage. It is already late for the human race to seriously introspect about its ways of life, development and acquisition that are denying posterity the very chance to exist and grow. The recent pandemic has given a new focus and orientation to the ongoing discussions and has also inspired writers to engage with the issue in novel and creative ways.

Humanity's power to degrade the environment has become unprecedentedly dangerous. In fact, we have already changed the environment irreversibly, and suicidally so. What we call nature is no longer nature in its pristine glory. Human intervention has transformed it into something sub- rather than semi-human: a combination of climate, topography, the original environment and the effects of the long history of human intervention. If it was agriculture that had transformed the landscape once, it is now urbanization that has affected the broader areas of our environment. Managing the environment is becoming a practical rather than a theoretical problem. It is not enough that we create theme parks or conserve a select few areas. 'Museumizing' nature and landscape will not be enough. Several animals and birds are on the verge of extinction; the list is growing, and human beings can easily be next in the at-risk list. What we require today is not isolated action, but concerted action at the global level. Techno-fascism that leads to eco-fascism—both have their roots in human greed and aggression—is one of the inevitable fall-outs of blind and unsustainable patterns of development.

The original sin perhaps, lies with the advocates of 'scientism' who wrote about 'conquering' nature. Thinkers like Francis Bacon and Rene Descartes were among the pioneers in creating an anti-nature philosophy and a reductive scientism through works like Bacon's *Novum Organum* and Descartes' *Discourse on Method*. Bacon used the language of violence, war and rape in addressing nature. In their anthropocentric arrogance, Bacon and Descartes, perhaps, did not realize that human beings can only collaborate with nature. We can discover nature's secrets and put them to human use; but if we try to 'conquer' her, she must wreak her revenge in the form of climate change, pollution, earthquakes, epidemics and floods that we are witnessing now. Adam Smith applied this greed to economics in his *Wealth of Nations*, where he argued that the selfish competition between individuals for the accumulation of wealth will ultimately lead to common good. Capitalism, with its 'open market' theory, built further on this instinct for individual possession and accumulation as against even distribution and collective management of wealth. The idea of 'conquest' was also linked to the actual conquest of lands, that led to colonial exploitation and the slavery of peoples and nations. Colonialism meant plunder, and it led to severe destruction of natural habitats and environments. The greedy and aggressive colonial 'gaze' turned our beautiful forests and landscapes into mere resources for revenue.

In *A Green History of the World*, Clive Ponting has traced our exploitative tendencies to ancient civilizations like Mesopotamia, Indus Valley and Rome, where deforestation and over-cultivation had a disastrous impact on the environment. In the post-industrial world, with its density of population, colonial exploitation and capital accumulation, the unscrupulous use of technology, unmoderated industrial development and the hegemony of economics over culture, have found a new and frightening acceleration.

Even in post-colonial nations, development is mechanically identified with a form of industrial growth that ignores the cultural and ethical dimensions of development. The concept has also impacted art, which is now being perceived as a commodity. Ernst Fischer, in his *Necessity of Art*, has qualified capitalism as a new King Midas that turns everything it touches into a commodity. Painting, sculpture, music, literature, theatre, cinema: nothing is an exception. Everything is a part of what Theodor Adorno termed 'culture industry', where culture is subjected to the law of capital and market. This is in keeping with Octavio Paz's observation that modernism in art and literature began as a reaction to capitalist modernity. It has failed to develop 'creative participation' as it celebrates the alienation of the individual from nature and society.

We need to overcome the dualist philosophy based on binaries and re-enchant the world with a holistic approach that interrogates the post-enlightenment belief that humans can create culture only by destroying nature. Art is organically linked to nature and derives its raw materials from nature. Only by reconnecting with nature and its wilderness, its myths and oral lore, and its eco-aesthetic principles, can we move forward to what the socialist-ecologist

David Pepper calls 'green postmodernism' where the material will no more be the antinomy of the spiritual, and individual happiness will not be the opposite of collective happiness.

The last fifty years have seen the development of an ecocritical philosophy that theorizes the intersections between writers, culture and our physical environment. Even though it was William Rueckert who introduced the term in *Literature and Ecology: An Experiment in Ecocriticism*, it was Joseph Meeker's *The Comedy of Survival: Literary Ecology and a Play Ethic* (1974) who first defined the subject. According to Meeker, literary ecology was concerned with the biological themes that appears in literature. Its aim was to discover the role of literature in human ecology. Literary works, Meeker suggests, often reveal beliefs about the truth of natural processes and the cultural ideologies that have brought our human race to the modern environmental crisis. Cheryll Glotfelty who edited the first Ecocriticism Reader, describes ecocriticism as an attempt to unravel the exchanges between nature and culture. It has one leg in literature: as a theoretical discourse, it connects equally with human and non-human beings. The writer's world is not only the social world, but the ecosphere itself. The earth, Glotfelty suggests, is at the centre of ecocriticism just as gender is at the centre of feminist and Marxist theories of class. Ecocriticism, according to Lawrence Buell, brings space into the critical agenda that has so far been confined to the theme, plot, and characters. He sees it as an umbrella term that embraces various modes and approaches. Sven Birkerts calls it 'egocriticism' as it re-reads literature to discover what it has to say about our egocentrism, greed and craze for wealth and power. Some ecocritics also draw strength from Engels' *Dialectics of Nature*, from Raymond Williams's insights into the city-country contradictions and from the works of Theodore Adorno, Walter Benjamin and other New Left thinkers.

The recent pandemic has intensified the call for a paradigm change in our self-awareness. Noam Chomsky points to the dangers of not keeping nature an organic part of common sense and human philosophy. Modernity has failed to understand the human–nature relationship in a holistic manner. We need to probe deeper into the thinking of the so-called 'primitive' or tribal communities. Nature does not do anything without purpose. Perhaps, we need to interrogate the old Enlightenment humanism whose emancipatory mission was defeated by instrumental rationality—as has been reiterated by Horkheimer, Adorno and Michel Foucault—a tradition that goes back to Spinoza and has inspired thinkers like Gilles Deleuze and Félix Guttari. What is called for is not a rejection of humanism, but the expansion of its intellectual and ethical territory. It is a structure, as Edward Said suggests in *Humanism and Democratic Criticism*, that we need to attain through the intervention of the human will and active subjectivity. Human beings have now become a geological force, and it is for us to move away from the transhumanist schemes to develop the species into a super-human ethereal power. We need to retrieve the lost continuity between natural history and human history and unlearn the histories where human beings are at the centre of everything and assumed to be the crown of creation. The Anthropocene Age demands a reworking of all our discourses as even objects and chemicals, from, hormones and enzymes to mood-altering drugs, can alter the human psyche. Artificial intelligence is no more mere science fiction. The old nature–culture binary has become obsolete. We need to know that our history is but a small chapter in the history of our planet and of evolution. Nature can exist without us as it had done before our emergence. Other living beings have their claim on the earth's resources that we plunder in the name of 'progress.' Slavoj Žižek points out how a virus has turned our bodies into mere photocopy machines. We need to redefine ethics and expand our understanding of equality, democracy, and posthumanism.

Writers, or *vates* by the old definition, have a leading role to play in sensitizing people to the impending environmental disasters through their writing and through their actions as concerned citizens. Our anthology, where poets from around the world look at these issues from multiple points of view and articulate their relationship with nature and the environment—tense, strained, harmonious, meditative, nostalgic—in a variety of poetic forms, aspires to be no more than a baby step in the articulation of a new aesthetic of survival. *Greening the Earth* is, in a sense, a sequel to *Singing in the Dark,* an anthology of poetry around the COVID-19 pandemic that we had co-edited in 2020. The two collections are related in subtle and not so subtle ways. The pandemic has brought to the fore ecological concerns that several thinkers and activists had already been talking about. We would like to thank Elizabeth Kuruvilla of Penguin Random House, India, who showed special interest in the book. Our gratitude to all the poets who generously contributed their poems with permission to include them.

The rich and diverse array of poetic voices that we have included here, grapple with the ongoing environmental crisis with their own kind of permeable thoughts, words and images. Within the polemics of literary debate, 'nature poetry' has had a bad rap with publishers until only a few decades ago when climate change became a real issue. While nature poetry has never been the exclusive domain of the Greek and Latin pastorals or the British Romantic poets, its true merit was diminished by the publishing industry in the twentieth century. It is only in the last decade or so that *Greening the Earth* has regained astonishing political currency and urgency. From being perceived as merely 'descriptive' in a pejorative sense, it has assumed a definite shift and rich political dimension as our often destructive relationship with our environment has become a hard reality. Connecting to mother earth through poetry and understanding the true worth of our environment through verse, has become important as the environmental crisis looms large amid all of humanity. The intricate connection with our ecosystem, with nature and our biosphere, seems fraught as humanity is threatened with extinction. The need for emissions reduction, the need to heed global warming, the need to recognize ourselves as thoughtless and greedy manipulators, has become overwhelming.

While a few poems in our anthology offer a perspective on how humans can respond to the reality of extinction, others give us an awareness of how we can struggle to keep what we still have. Some poems share earnest insights into our own evolution, and others offer grim warnings or raise voices against the imminent threat of extinction and the fate of our planet. Some poets spin interconnected incantations and weave healing nature through their blood, and others honor it by connecting the sustainable with their personal poetic bones. The environmental theme of most poems can inspire meditation as well as a commitment to apocalyptic action. The poets anthologized here offer landscapes of beauty and joy, of rustic retreat, of communion with our natural world, against the larger looming questions of human survival, of spurring towards conservation and preservation, of recognizing our ancestral knowledge, of a complicated pact and a complex impact.

The anthology, in short, is our kind of shock tactic to the glaring lacunae within our urbanized, post-industrial society. What distinguishes us further, is that our anthology is a global chorus of poetic voices. We cannot stress enough the 'sustainable' route felt in the 'sustainable' poetic voices of our anthology. Along with our conscious ecowarrior poets, *Greening the Earth* is our kind of responsible activism.

As editors, we have taken our own decision to retain the American English and British English as used by individual poets from across the globe. We have organized the poems alphabetically, in order to avoid any hierarchical suggestions concerning our esteemed ecopoets and green poets.

K. Satchidanandan and Nishi Chawla

Atacama

Abhay K.

I am here
amidst this immensity
of the cold desert,
shadows leaping out
windmills inviting
new Don Quixotes
hills rolling out and curved
supple breasts of the desert
Sun shining ever bright
in silence
not a single animal or bird,
nothing like Earth

ii
in the vastness of the desert
the road merely a line

snowcapped Andes
sibylline as ever

iii
at dawn
the moon hanging
from the sky
like a sickle
stars still bright
on the way to Lagunas Altiplánicas

iv
little hills along the Andes
like camelids' humpbacks
sunrise
lights them up in soft pink

v
an inverted pyramid
of light, air, sky, clouds
in the Laguna Miñiques
on its bleached shores
of salt
Kutz birds' nest.

Imagine

Shanta Acharya

The song of humpbacked whales,
breath of life flowing through conch shells,

uniquely decorated flukes falling on waves,
huge white flippers slapping the water.

Imagine a grizzly bear on its haunches
in the bend of the river scooping up silver slivers,
tossing minnows into its yawning mouth.

Forests, canyons, rivers, waterfalls, double rainbows,
the laughter of lightning holding us in thrall.

Blush of a bride, the sky at sunrise, sunset,
spreading in wild abandonment.

Imagine cloud formations of changing configurations,
dove white to crow black, altocumulus to tornado chasers.

Smile of a camel filling the loneliness of a desert,
a cheetah in motion, the dance of King Cobras.

Sighing of leaves when the wind gives them a shake,
hawks soaring on tides of air, wild wings streamlined.

A colony of bats singing, meditating upside down
on an ancient tree grown large as a grandparent.

The majesty of a reclusive snow leopard disappearing
in a blizzard on the slopes of Mount Everest.

A smoking volcano blowing spectacular hoops
of fire, pouring molten lava for days,
depositing ash on the tray of land.

Imagine a stately cavalcade of moving mountains of ice
in the Arctic, shimmering with the aurora borealis.

Brightly coloured wings of a butterfly hovering,
their translucency in moonlight revealing . . .

Now open your eyes wide and imagine
our rich world bereft of nature's blessing.

Grant us the wisdom to survive—
like trees that live long, enriching the planet;
loyal protectors of the realm, standing firm,
asking nothing in return of heaven or earth.

Grant us the wisdom to imagine—
the need to give and forgive, not merely receive,
like an oyster transforming grit into pearl,
the giving growing, becoming something precious.

Grant us the wisdom to rejoice—
a long time after we are returned to earth, the lives
we leave behind may cherish the fruits of our action:
a million species saved from extinction.

Grant us the wisdom to love—
love without limit, love that casts a widening
circle of light for the world to walk forward in,
singing the songs of its forgotten springs.

Grant us the wisdom to pray—
strive to set right the injustices we perpetuate,
courage to change the things that must be changed,
else there will be nothing left to live for.

In memory of Rydal Mount

Usha Akella

Bard of Nature, one year ago I was on your land
looking upon an emerald accordion
tumbling toward a river,
awed by a tiered resplendence of magnolias
and sky-sweeping trees,
I understood how you moved in a minutia of signs:
rock, cataract, grass, lakes, mountain, vale and humanity—one,
you heard the music of one in another.

Nature is this wallet of green outside my window,
small change, this paradise, my garden of Eden
a constellation of neighborhoods, yards like slabs of biscuits,
we are denizens of the city,
hordes of ants bustling in make-believe,
lives clocked by fb likes, a sitcom's upcoming season
more dependable than Nature's erratic dousing,
the *fever of the world* is our normal,
my forest, these oak trees of alligator-bark,
my seasons modestly pass here on this street,
trees cast umbra and penumbra of shadows,
grass furiously knits in the wind,
in the amber light each evening trees darken,
children bike about on the yellow
oak pollen-soot-spattered tongue of driveways,
cicadas whirr crazily—the sound of silence in the evening.
There! A squirrel stands on tiptoe, his elongated body taut,
he nibbles at something between his paws,

abruptly stops; on fours, he scampers tipsily
forward, backward . . . a lost pedestrian looking for an address.

We know nothing of diurnal rhythms,
urban-bred, our children dye hair purple and blue,
and roiling papaya sunsets go unwatched from the window,
we do not smell the air to say, spring is here!
Smell the scent of roses before they bloom
or know when the bluebonnets
will cascade the highway's grass,
the monsoon brings no chant of mystery,
we don't look at the alphabet of the moon
and predict a woman's child-bearing,
we don't read the clouds for rain,
don't feel home in our veins,
the world around greets us a stranger,
we rise and fall with a cacophonous sun,
we crack apart like a veined tarmac,
Nature never did betray till she is betrayed.

Ghost Fox and Spirit Seal

Joel Allegretti

After Edgar Allan Poe

GHOST FOX: Ghost Fox?

SPIRIT SEAL: Arctic Fox is your past name, as Ringed Seal is mine. Here I'm Spirit Seal.

GHOST FOX: Where is *here*?

SPIRIT SEAL: Where you and I are now. Where the world that disowned us isn't.

GHOST FOX: I remember the world. You were my prey there.

SPIRIT SEAL: Nothing is prey here.

GHOST FOX: I remember Killer Whale.

SPIRIT SEAL: Specter Whale.

GHOST FOX: Musk Ox.

SPIRIT SEAL: Ghost Ox.

GHOST FOX: Reindeer.

SPIRIT SEAL: Apparition Deer.

GHOST FOX: I remember meals of seabirds.

SPIRIT SEAL: I remember meals of polar cod.

GHOST FOX: I remember ice.

SPIRIT SEAL: The ice changed into water. Slowly.

GHOST FOX: Miles of ice.

SPIRIT SEAL: Decades of slowly. Then *slowly* changed into *finally*.

What I Found in My Grave

Sarah Allen

i.

The end of the world is never permanent.
No 'should haves', only 'did haves'.
The rest is ephemera not capable
of supporting human life.
Forever is chemical.
The end of the world is only as
permanent as fall and thunder.
A cat winks and what have we learned?
The end of the world is when you close
your eyes, and open them again.

ii.

The moon has died, let us
bury her.
The moon said she'd buy
the flowers herself
for the funeral and now
she's gone, the Cheshire smile,
the full full full,
the one small step
gone. I keep going
in and out, in and out
feasting on glowing
from the buffet table.
The moon had no cousins.

The moon slept in her own bed.
We bury the moon
but the moon does not
fit underground.

iii.

I am floating today.
My shoes have fallen off
and now my ribs are loose.
We are about to lose ourselves
but hold on. Flight
is the only way to reach
the center of
the earth.

iv.

Did Icarus fly too near, or
was it the Sun in love
with Icarus? Shall we forgive
the Sun its impatience
to finally feel what it's always
shone its light on?
Does the Sun deserve
a chance to rise and to
fall and fall and fall?

v.

the bones I died in
and the ones I'm not coming back for.

fluids I can't take on board,
weapons that won't make it through customs.
somewhere between my ribs is a notice
of inspection that begins
to protect your fellow passengers . . .

Touching the Ground*
(Earth Day, 1990)

Michael Anania

I

Nothing we know of seems
more certain than this,
the struggle of the leaf

against the bud, the first
pale heart of lilac, box
elder and locust tree

quickening, ailanthus,
the tree of heaven,
splitting the sidewalk

once again. Clouds rush
eastward, a chill rain
clamours off the prairie

and subsides, and it is April
everywhere, like a green
swell breaking into air.

---

* From *Selected Poems* (1994), originally written for and published by the
Parliament of the World's Religions.

II

This is the ring of roses,
this is the barefoot dance,
the first place of mystery

we offer to the gods,
the breathless circle
and the deep heart's core,

the earth's first green
wind-flexed into the light,
sea grass and sea anemone,

the melting edge of mountain
snow, soft rainforest humus,
an airborne orchid snared

in prairie grass, salt surge
through coral, the granite
fissure composed with pine.

III

Ashes, ashes and a burning
rain, half-lives in ground
water, the air made bitter

in a bitter trade—forest
sold, river entailed,
whale bartered for a plastic

grocery sack, molluscs scattered
like small change, birds
bargained for feathers,

prairies for asphalt, otters
for oil, ourselves for gasoline.
Ashes, ashes—the grit

that catches in our throats,
compounds we exchange
for the enzyme and the gene.

IV

All growth grows on what
has grown. The circle of water,
the circle of air, the great

circles of plant and soil,
the blue circumference of sky
converge in the green space

of a single leaf. Between
leaf vein and leaf's edge
the earth offers itself

and its long history, a green
coincidence balanced briefly
on the planet's stem, stipuled

to our fingers and our eyes.
It is neither wilderness nor park.
But ourselves we celebrate and save.

King of the Forest*

Issath Rehana Mohamed Azeem (Anar)

Beyond the hills
You rise up and grow
Replacing the sun
You remain seated
Keeping aside the snow-capped peaks
With thick green, curly heads
The wood of my love has turned thick
Declaring to be the sovereign of the wood
You penetrate to the tip of the roots
With glittering rays
Rule over me with exhilarating embrace
Like a river
I roll down the curved paths
The wings are with you
You fly away
Clutching with all the clefts
Our poems
Browse all through the wilds
The brightness and the song of the one
Who got in
Opens the locks
With a gentle warmth
Hereafter
The winds the king has sliced open
Will shower flowers all over my forest
And smell sweet till the sunset.

---

* Translated from the Tamil by Prof. Thanga Jayaraman

Todi

In the morning my mother becomes a forest
Scented with the sacred sounds of *Todi*.
Mystic women sit beneath her trees
With closed eyes,
Their *tanpuras* pregnant
With the music
Whose birth raises the sun,
Seducing it in the depths of gloom,
Undressing its luminous body with grace.

The sun, coquettish,
Sweeps the mists away,
And the sunlight
Embracing the leaves
Defines love, defies death.

In the forest the trees speak Awadhi,
Though here, words don't matter.
It's the music which speaks—
About the harmony,
And what the winds scatter.

In the morning
My mother becomes a forest
Whose trees are engraved
With an ancient language
Which can only be spoken
By a stringed instrument

That lets you slide
From one note
To another.

This journey, glissando,
Is not how we walked
Between rooms,
Plucking moments
Of our adolescence, our
Sorrows and laughter,
The clamors
Of a strange weather.

This journey
Between musical notes,
Buried in the language
Engraved on the tree trunks
Of the forest
That my mother becomes
In the morning
When the mystics sing *Todi*,
Is the time
We did not live
Together.

Dream*

Subhro Bandopadhyay

In a cloudy courtyard of mud, broken mirrors and conches stayed implanted in the brain. Our running away was towards an unclear literacy; steadily disappearing civets and black monitor lizards; even when we saw the water steadily rise without the tidal call, we stayed mum—as if the destination were the final word and not the journey

Coming to your land I see *Gwaelod*, a Bronze Age forest turned to stone under the sea—your ancient tales speak of *Seithenyn* who opened the floodgates; and there, the deluge, the devouring sea. I see fossilized mangroves with aerial roots; water steadily swallowing heights, far from potability and people, plastic has never turned to stone under the sea

---

* Translated from the Bengali by Sampurna Chattarji
The mangrove forest in the Gangetic delta is one of the most threatened places on Earth because of climate change that results in rising levels of sea water.

Walking, I pass

Jennifer Barber

a gray house, a fence,

a blue house with yellow
flowers by the door.

I can't get a breath of air,

heat gathers in the crown
of an oak, the verse

in Ezekiel where God
says to pick up coals,

scatter them over the city,
sow the light of reckoning.

I cross without looking, a driver
hits the brakes hard,

around the corner, noon

falls on a copper beech—
it fires up each glossy leaf.

Plant Growth*

Ricardo Bellveser

A Gonzalo Santonja
The stone is a forehead
where dreams moan
FGL

I don't know how much time I've spent
to study the growth of this site,
I also look at the trees and gladioli,
the enredded rose bushes and their roots
and I feel like rosemary.
This tree, judging by its appearance,
his silence and his stillness, does not grow,
nor does this balancing branch,
nor does the magnolia grow.
We should pay more attention to it.
to these things, to perceive the aroma
enclosed in the city walls
containing the life of the stones,
to understand how plants move
and to see the tenderness in the granite face
cheeks subjected to the wind that kisses them.

I walk the trails,
among the sources arrested
in flawless glass jets,

---

* From *Jadines*
  Translated from the Spanish by Nishi Chawla

the weightlessness of the beautiful insects,
the soil of the roots that sharpen it,
the lights between the leaves.
I know these walls grew centuries ago,
here the stones have been educated

by the hammer, and his scraping
it's windy and the cold takes care
to silence them with arrogant resignation.

Everything grows here with a human rhythm,
because even if we look at the back of our hands
we don't see them change. But they change.
That's the secret of this movement,
that is not perceived. We only understand
that time has passed, when
everything stops and all of a sudden winter comes.

Two Strokes of Red

Oscar René Benítez

She painted me brightly colored dreams
in the endless canvas of a blue sky.

Tender looks, verses; all her poetry;
landscape transformed into a woman.
Two touches of deep red
her sweet lips
and in her mouth, bloomed poetry and song.

What enchanted mystery locked inside her eyes
in the charming spell of her gaze?

Rhythm, sensuality, beauty and sin.
Oh the sweetness of her voice liquid and tender
like Ulysses, dragging me to a wreck!

And in my chest she left forever
a magical disturbing concern.
A love without age, time or distance
wrapped in days, nights and blue hours.

I come back to seek in her gaze
the dying light of setting suns,
the blue dreams that we weaved together
and promises of love that we did not deliver.

But today
I just leave for her

this bunch of silences
for days that without seeing her elapsed.
This handful of sighs that bloomed
in the cold and long dawns without her.

The Perception of Beauty Is a Moral Test*

Joanie Puma Bennet

'You shouldn't buy my house,' I tell the quirky,
lost man when he reads me his late wife's poem from
the funeral program in his pocket. I read mine
about the night sky; that's deep, he says, weighted.

Cozy two-bedroom south-facing cottage boasts
beautiful 90-year-old oak floors. Very
green: no ac, no dryer, no dishwasher,
no cable. Passive solar, winter sun—God's
SAD light—pours into living room, dining room,
kitchen, porch. Bald eagles glide over clotheslines.
Big trees; semi-rural; creek three houses down.
Clearly it's a Thoreau house. Very private.

Dismissed as a fizzbo†
by local real estate mafia, too low
a state for even Sparticus to emerge,
invisible or caught in their mean crosshairs.
Panic now avoid the rush: last month buried
St. Joseph under the hammock, called neighbor
realtor (bound for Bali), stuffed red envelope
in fluffy snowbank, worst of all, dropped the price.

No sage, sweet grass smudging ritual blessing
the sweet house healed me through two decades of strife

---

* Henry David Thoreau
† FSBO (for sale by owner)

while I wasn't looking. And I know Thoreau
would live here if he had to live in town.

'It is life near the bone that is the sweetest,'*
coos an unfamiliar tenor as the door
opens and in strides Henry David Thoreau.
'Oh My Gosh!' I gasp. 'She with one breath attunes
the spheres, and also my human heart,'† he sighs.

'It's taking so long to sell my house!' I blurt.
'What should I do?' 'Do? You might start packing. Just
as "the bluebird carries the sky on his back,"‡
you'll know your course by the ruffle of the wind.'

'But it's taking time, and I—' 'As if you could
kill time without injuring eternity.'§
It'll happen.' 'But there's no one who truly
appreciates my house except you.' 'I am a parcel of
vain strivings tied by a chance bond together.'¶

'But I do like this house. "Most of the luxuries,
and many of the so-called comforts, of life
are not only not indispensable, but
positive hindrances to the elevation of mankind."**
I'll take it!' he exclaims, opening his purse.

---

*   Henry David Thoreau
†   Henry David Thoreau
‡   Henry David Thoreau
§   Henry David Thoreau
¶   Henry David Thoreau
** Henry David Thoreau

Tree*

Richard Berengarten

*The tree of life groweth with slow and
steady increase through unmeasured time*

Basilides of Alexandria

Tree planted
in my core
spreading growing
tree of songs
many branched
flame tree
rooted in death
blood bathed
breath blown
bone fibred
body tree
elemental
tree in a seed

---

* Written at 20 Tenison Avenue, Cambridge, 1978–79, as a response
to Ann Waldman's chant-poem, *Fast Speaking Woman*. *Tree* was first
published by Menard Press, London, in 1981. It has been reprinted many
times and been translated into a dozen languages. It forms the core of
the online *Albero Project* : http://www.margutte.com/?p=23972&lang=en.
This poem, *Tree*, has the same number of lines as a year has days. This
makes it three lines longer than the height, in feet, of the tallest tree in
the world, the coastal Redwood Howard Libbey Tree in Humboldt State
Park, California. The Californian tree should have caught up by now.
The epigraph is from C.G. Jung, *Septem Sermones ad Mortuos* (tr. H.G.
Baynes, Stuart & Watkins, London, 1961). *Basilides* was C.G. Jung's
pseudonym.

full throated
thousand tongued
thick skinned
creaking tree
enduring thunder
wind eroded
snow bound
survivor tree
skeletal
under storm clouds
budding slow
through despair
thrusting hopes
of high skies
cirrus strewn
milky ways
and birds returning
wakening
sleep laden tree
circled in memories
close grained
springwood
and summerwood
tree of dreams
and visitations
leaved with hair
of fallen heroes
snake wreathed
giant guarded
threaded with voices
and children's laughter
ancestor tree

earth drinking
sky swallowing
bowelled living
grave tree
light eating
pillar of wisdom
of smoke of cloud
desert beacon
whorled tornado
fire fountain
golden chain
leading the way
through night
with agate jet
and haematite
from evening
gathering emerald
carnelian
and diamond dews
and in the studded
bowl of dawn
with pearl and opal
dissolving them
spreadeagled
against the morning
a scented trellis
spanning noon
blue crowned
tree of earth
water fire
of air of airs
light ship

dusky barge
sailing on
wind seasoned
around year ends
and back again
clay moored
soil harboured tree
prow lapped
by heaven's tides
sun cradle
moon basket
cloud blanketed
cask of stars
rocking meteors
shaking planets
ploughing galaxies
on long oars
world hammering
sky raking
word breaking
rocksplitting tree
bone-cracking
wrist of boughs
tower of strength
pivot fulcrum
axial roof tree
probing pharos
ever turning
clawed through crust
of cliff and crag
pointed dactyl
spark igniting

flame hurling
quill clutched
in a stone fist
illuminating
day's page
in green and gold leaf
manuscript
chiselling plaques
in night's crypt
with serifs inked
in baryons
kindling speech
of origins
to sing darkness's
molten core
of ice
moss and coal
fossil fern
and dinosaur
time tree
revolving burning
prising open
history's lips
drilling its jaws
to spit pips
needle twigs
and wiry shoots
earthed in its seams
and blood routes
ore flowers
on brittle stems
magnetic amber

diadems
electric tree
lightning conductor
energy funnel
through stratospheres
chimney built
in the pot of death
fuelling years
with quiet breath
tree of creation
tree of destruction
temple planted
in an upturned skull
worming woody
fibres through
eye socket
and mandible
world tree
scroll keeping
cave covered
by sky mountain
joy tent pitched
in wilderness
dome whispering
spire trembling
gargoyle gnarled
buttress of hills
glory cone
mist piercing
latticed steeple
nesting angels
fan vaulted

echoing tree
runged ladder
for the soul's fingers
valved throat
winged glottis
ringing singing
ribcage tree
harmonising
forest airs
and air of plains
in symphony
with the unceasing
ocean fend
orchestral baton
dowser's rod
dipping bending
greenwood sapling
bowed by longing
flex of hope
tightrope stretched
from loam to God
tuned wand
alembic
caduceus twined
branching vessel
thermometer measuring
ages' heat
mercurial sap
rising falling
hollow tree
fluted with stomata
wooden well

mine tunnelled
bell cord
and lungs of Hades
gale harness
fanning the damned
and the twice dead
and the never born
with harp tinkling
in glen and glade
and lament of orchards
for Hesperides
womb tree
moist lipped
rain collecting
underground tree
resin caulked
wine vat
tree of desire
taboo fruited
mountain spring
orgy scented
waterfall
weeping tree
flooded river
magma breasted
lava tree
sowing islands
eddying delta
coral tree
perpetually blazing
deciduous
tree of madness

tree of passion
set with thorns
sweating blood
pain tree
evergreen
showering ghosts
shedding children
common tree
brittle old
crowded stunted
overshadowed tree
insect gnawed
rot infected
lightning blasted
husk of famine
raped mutilated
people's tree
obelisk
dead tree
uprooted felled
sawn plank
hearth tree
for warmth and fuel
table tree
for bread and wine
architraved
thyrsus totem
bound and staked
earthed and fused
blood spattered
royal trunk
nailing hell

to paradise
gallows tree
rising again
knuckled knotted
blind man's staff
swordblade
heavy hilted
thick boled
ivory tusk
ebony spear
erect conquering
tree in a prairie
in a city garden
pruned and tended
by patient hands
quiet tree
of yes of no
of this of that
of black of white
confluence
of pasts and futures
rooted in ever
praising now
flesh tree
rimmed in muscle
blood and sweat
sighing shivering
shuddering tree
generous
sperm tree
life pump
ever brimming

around whose roots
the serpent coils
around whose branches
flits the white bird
tree of spirits
tree of secrets
buried in heaven
to flower through veins
arteries nerves
capillary tree
meristematic
your tap root drowned
in infinite skies
I descend up
and ascend down
rod of aeons
of Adam Kadmon
Jesse David
and Sataniel
and Moses
on the high mountain
Buddha tree
Tilopa tree
zen tree
tantric tree
Kali's tree
dancing on skulls
volcanic tree
of Ashtaroth
Lilith
Ishtar and Astarte
nurturing

moss and lichen
mould gathering
mushroom tree
mother of orchids
and mistletoe
tree of Dryads
tree of Druids
where the spider weaves
and the rooks nest
and the bat flitters
and the kestrel waits
tree of lives
of consciousness
generative
language tree
speaking names
telling stories
histories
transformations
depthless tree
deathless tree
tree of comrades
of airs I breathe
unpruned
untameable
immortal tree
overarching
freedom tree
tree of love
tree of justice
human rainbow
blossoming

The Awakening*

Tara Bergin

better

he remembered the dreams he had had
as he lay there in fever and delirium
in the last days of Lent and Eastertide
during the latter days of Lent and Easter week
during the end of Lent and Holy Week
when he dreamt of a *sickness* on the streets of Hotan
when he dreamt of a *sickness* on the streets of Moscow
when he dreamt of a *sickness* on the streets of Lahore
and saw the fabric of life unravelling
when he saw the whole world desolated

only children moving through the dreamworld
brothers fleeing from burning buildings
the older brother passing down the younger brother
the younger brother jumping from the older brother's arms
whole villages and towns
whole cities and populations
washing their hands
covering their faces

but somewhere in the back of the dream
somewhere in the back of the dream
salmon flew from their nets

---

* The opening lines of this poem are based on different translations of
Dostoevsky's *Crime & Punishment*

falcons swam from their chains
forests of ash and sycamore
awoke from a coma in a kind of re-birth
and saw their whole lives
in a different way

Shelter in Place

Charles Bernstein

It's no go from the get
go, strumming a mordant
medley from the old days
when we danced with
abandon. Now we are
abandoned, God's
silence deafens us
to each other, and the
fiddlers diddle a
familiar tune. Familiar
and deadly. Wake
up say those still
still small voices:
the Anthrobscene
is playing just north
of here and this is
just a taste of
what's to come.

The sand attracts just about more than any girl or boy could dream
On the lone shore after the apocalypse. Vans race'round with
    bracing
Theatrics and I sit back and think about lost riverbeds where I
    buried
My thoughts before the storm began or is it *begun* or maybe it
    never
Really happened and there is just this beach, this ocean of regret,
    this

Mascaraed sky. I reach out to you every day but I know it's too late.
The anthropocene is the delusion of a bathetic interloper scratching
Obscene slogans on the melting ice.

Extinction

Maren Bodenstein

here
on the prairie we measure
the years
by the extinction of insects
that visit our porch lamps
the brittle
longhorn is gone
for a while now the giant
stick insect no longer
flares its scarlet wings even
the bluewhite chafers have succumbed
to the heat
by day we dwell in the creek
my sisters and I
one of us pregnant
but I keep forgetting
if it is me
look I am full term now
I tell them stroking my flat belly
on the horizon
a fire roars
through the grasses and over
the houses it marches
the last army of insects
into the bellies of storks
a confusion of vehicles
full of belongings flees
towards us

Ma in her car
with the poodle
comes rushing at us
get in she shouts
misses the bridge
plunges deep
we must rescue her
I tug at the metal
but my sisters
heavy with chatter
do not hear
Ma broken mermaid sneezes
opens her blue-eyes
happy
to see me

Iceland, Summer

Rafaella Del Bourgo

Returning to the apartment I rented in Reykjavik,
I drive west past the fishing village of Hofn,
its channel to be navigated with care
due to the shifting patterns of the shoals.
The rocking boats, and the seafarers,
safe, for now, in the harbor.

To the edge of Jokulsarlon, the bay
where the glacier calves off into icebergs,
some small as travel trunks,
a few the size of a room.
Some are a celestial blue, some are banded
with dark streaks of volcanic dust.

The lagoon water licks at them;
the tidal pull draws them slowly
under the bridge
and, much diminished,
they sail off to be lost at sea.

Past the black sand beach at Dyrholaey
with its lava pillars rising up from the water,
and an arch stretching out past the waves,
which gives the area its name:
'the hill-island with the door-hole.'

Two a.m. I return to my temporary home.
I push aside heavy drapes to see how

the 'midnight sun,'
paints snow-capped
mountains to the north
with a light, relentless and alien.

Road-weary, overwhelmed
by the landscape—at times
bleak, at times beautiful,
always unfamiliar—
I collapse on the couch.
Crawling into my lap,
the resident cat I agreed
to care for during my visit.
Like my tom back home,
he is heavy and orange,
brushes his face against my hand.

I lean my head back.
I am a visitor here,
far from my home port.
This cat is my anchor.

I Don't Know if You Saw

Coral Bracho

I don't know if you saw that documentary
where the vast meadow
in which they held us started closing.
One fence then another, and another, one
piece then another, a gap
and another, one door to another
smaller door, a corridor, and there
they were, weighing us, measuring us. I don't know
if you.
In their place.
At the exact angle. The instrument
at that exact moment.
Each one
and the next, the chop, in their place,
on the knee, on the hip, an exact slice,
the thigh,
a cut, and another,
the belly, a hook,
the ribs,
and another,
a hook
and the chain and another. Everybody,
all of us there.

Daydream

Ann Bracken

No one needs an excuse to scroll back to a gentler season,
to a place in time where I can abandon the pell-mell
pace of living I've embraced for so long.
I'm dreaming of planting my feet
in a clear stream at the end
of my driveway.

In the field by the brook, sheep wear bells creating
a moving symphony as they graze among a
riot of day lilies. I find it no more absurd
to fete such a simple flower

than it is for the fairies in my daughter's
book to gather tufts of moss
for their cushions.

Beholden

Erin Holtz Braeckman

I come to you as Crow. But not before you first come to me. My bones are left like tinder in the dark ashes of my feathers when you find them. Crouching low in the crisp clutch of Spring the way the grandmothers once did, you speak words of ritual from the cave of folk memory you've walked right into without knowing. And you ask—before you hear my totem call from the pines high overhead; you ask before you slip one of my bones into your pocket. Because wrapped inside the song of that old teaching circle you stepped within was this telling: what you collect, you become the caretaker of. Not the thing itself, but its living story. Those crystals on your altar? You are the steward of their mountains. Those shells lining your windowsill? You are the custodian of their oceans. The pressed petals and dried acorns and vials of sand—the bones; in them there are entire fields and forests and feral ones of whom you are a curator. Which is why I come to you this time, a cackle-caw of shade-shifters stalking through your sister spruces. The others fly when you near, leaving me below in the corner fencing, the wing you took the bone from a tangle of black shadow throwing back the light. I feel the moment you are beholden, Crow-Keeper; how you fold the wild beating of my body into your hands, placing me like a stone on a cairn into the bracken beyond; how those grandmothers come to braid feathers into your hair.

When the Dam Comes Down

Peter Brown

A fractal at first, the crackling slabs,
the rebar gathering noisy in the trees,
and flickering lights, Toyotas, ski boots, skis,
all the way down the slaloming canyon;

The mole trembles under the mud
as a fox, a goose, and a jungle gym
go swerving before the detonation
as the tonnage accumulates its din;

in gravity was the burden of damage
and now no further distinctions figure
between weight and mass and motion.
Everything you've known already done,

every staircase, window case,
pillowcase, pillow, earphone, iPhone,
each I-love-you, every devotion,
all the way down the slamming canyon.

Only the sun is high and the sky blue,
only the milkweed spores let loose
like milky stars afloat in the spray
above the cliffs, making their way.

I will Puncture this Boat

Tsead Brunja

I'm lying in a fold-out garden chair on our roof terrace
during something that feels like a late summer
it's august and my evening is all cloud air and sound
an aeroplane flies overhead
followed by its exhaust trail

mankind is leaving deep white marks on a blue pinhead

people with low-income often live shorter lives
in twenty years' time richer folk will be living here

a moped breaks
a front door opens
a lid bangs shut
the moped leaves

and we are safer healthier and richer than ever before

children are shouting commands and insults at each other
their voices running from one end of the street
to the other

*

a blackbird lands on the fence of another terrace
whenever it seems to have found a melody
it cuts its song short

with outstretched hands wind pushes a boat
through the treetops in the park
leaves tickling the keel

down in the street the children
are loud and boisterous
their enthusiastic screams swelling up
like a furious swarm of bees

the work their parents do for a living
has to become cheaper

they want their music to be free

we're constructing ceilings
while we should be working on our view

we're keeping ourselves
hungry servile and lost

a neighbor is practising his scales on a trumpet
I'm hurling curses at his open window

I'm part of an investment
a face in a portfolio

these poems are worth less
than my share in the statistics
the bodies I swipe to the right
the discount deals I'm suckered into

a mosquito buzzes above my head

in ethiopia an american president
praised the growing middle class
and their noble entrepreneurship

growth markets for high fructose corn syrup
ketchup soda and chicken

africa is on the move he says
happy he doesn't have to sing
for once

inside our neighbors kitchen a blender pulverizes
vegetables and fruit into juice
for the children

*

and we can't die because we are needed
some companies just can't do without us

a cheeky rose-ringed parakeet flies off
trying to screech his gang of thieves
out of the trees

in a san francisco suburb students are taught
the strength of being quiet collectively
by the david lynch foundation

their focus is improving
there are less fights
than before
will they still remember these lessons

when they're pecking and scratching
out a living by applying for a string
of small jobs?

you'll find vitamin fuck you in starlight
as well as in the darkness surrounding them

while we should be working on a view
we're building a roof for the sun to prey upon

to redesign the world we need to go back in time
back to the patient man etherized by corn coke and soap
spread out on a table underneath a roof

we'll teach him to work on a view
of paying attention and really being there

*

we're building a roof
we're adjusting nature we believe
she must be the patient

we're constructing a ceiling
turning compulsory education
into compulsory down payments
our students into owners of debt extra hands
for the long handle bellows of venture capital

illegal immigrants with academic titles
are not allowed to participate
but they've got to live somewhere

someone has to design their dirty house
and who will keep it clean?

doing your own work is forbidden
you might think you've got a future here
even though our work is getting cheaper
they're our jobs and not yours
we'll give them to the polish people
we choose

on a balcony someone drops a spoon
someone drops a plate

evolution you're born with short arms
karma too short to even reach the top shelf
you'll accept it

one of our neighbors' daughter
is having dinner with the neighbors next door
she makes items of food come to her
by singing their names

like a slow-moving circular saw a moped
removes itself from our block and the park
cutting up two worlds of sound

the voices of the children in the street
fighting over breadcrumbs like seagulls
are becoming louder faster higher louder
and then go quiet for a moment

*

the wind grabs the leaves of the small trees on the terrace first
then the branches so it can shake the leaves
even harder

and a child yells get on your bike and ride-ride

the wind ruffles through the tree crowns
through the park's lulling horizon

cutlery is being piled up on a plate
a spoon is being hit against a pan repeatedly
to make the food come off

a pair of little claws land on our metal fence
light litte bird's legs

it's Friday night
there's a bigger chance of that machine being a hair dryer
than a vacuum cleaner

the children laugh
I'm searching for a new brand a new kind of politics
and wonder if that was my wife in the kitchen just now
whether her steps on the stairs should be the last sound
you would be hearing in this poem

but there she is already
she asks me what I am doing
cuts and chews her food

*

pigeon wings are flapping
the children are getting back into their game
they are the loudest

after them come the mopeds
after those the neighbor's cutlery

and tomorrow we will be eating our mortgages
we'll be happy with our small debts
kneeling down on our brittle bones

for mercy
and tear gas

my wife lifts up her knee and touches the table
making it squeak and shift a little

I come from an area of knife stabbers
who on a Sunday afternoon
roll their cigarette butts from one corner
of their mouth to another
and then remove a dent from the side
of their drunken vauxhall cavallier
with bare hands

you have to climb on board
keep your mouth shut and your eyes on the road
and the billboards

because we might have made it
but our children haven't yet

I'm working on a view on my roof terrace
a view that will not be a ceiling
I'm about to puncture this boat before they send us back

A Warm Spell

Blake Campbell

Why these cloudless days of sun?
Why the catkins on the birch
Where the northern cardinals perch?
February isn't done.

Why the iris shoots that break
Through the earth two months too soon?
Why this humid afternoon?
Blue jays, sensing no mistake.

Only plenitude, call out
In the backyard and the park.
Thirsty voices after drought,

Would that you too could proclaim
New emissions of that spark
Doubt has hastened into flame.

Mother's Day Ft. Lincoln Cemetery

Kenneth Carroll

the osprey swim the skies above
the graves of mothers

invasive flowers bloom
hallow ground fertilized by longing

The osprey make their way
to the ancient river

Where they find others, broken-
hearted, silent as wings gliding

consoled by the knowing
that earth itself is a mother
its embrace loving, capacious
as blue skies

Green

Susana H. Case

After removal of the tumor
enables her to see
the color green for the first time,

she thinks cheese, moon,
azalea leaves, the soft pulp
of honeydew, parrots,

sculpted copper roofs,
the dulled sunfish
she saw years ago in Mexico.

She gazes anew at the starred
ceiling of Grand Central,
algae-green with grime.

Spring continues to stray toward
silence. The over-population
bomb grows more alarming.

Soon enough she will lie
under a quilt of grass,
its roots and borders tended to

by others. She wonders
if her grandchildren
will see anything left green.

To the Beauty of This Place

Grace Cavalieri

The land is telling its truth again.
After Winter's sharp sleep, it shows
what must be saved. Look at these

trees feathered with light,
the necklaces of foliage,
here from earth's compassion.

Now a harmony of place where
presidents, poets, shepherds and kings
talk of peace as they walk these paths.

While it's true there's no scale to measure
treasures, this one is of new water, new green
kept safe from the aridity of stricken places

and destruction's deadly face.
Instead, there's serenity here to pray against such visions.
'Hope' is the map that extends

under our house of sun,
where natural worlds thrive.
Just look at the surface of this earth

where we've come together, in the radiance
of all this flowering.

Kairos*

Priya Sarukkai Chabria

There is no news

. . . that on the shore of the known and
the unknown 33 waves wash my feet

as 33 hundred million gods
pour blessings that don't reach

us agitating for free speech
nor the 33 migrants clinging

to a raft, salt-bloated
within the boat of your eye

as you try to make
your body still as a bowl of stars

floating in the sea
we know exists but don't see
as it spins in Chronos

that was, is and will be
has dissolved and remade itself
33 billion times before

* First published in *NO NEWS 90 Poets Reflect on a Unique BBC Newscast*,
Eds. Paul Munden, Alvin Pand, Shanre Strange, Recent Work Press,
2020

for this is no news

no signals from within
no stutters from space
to tell us we aren't alone

in the way each tree
comes into being in the dark
in soil and sleep

as microscopic whisker
seeking life other
than itself that it needs to survive

probing air between
earth moist or not, that teems
with mycorrhizal fungi connecting blind

nor reprieve from
the signet ring whose each glint
melts jaws frames flesh
chips cables that gird the globe

there is no news

of the light emitted
by bones in the dark
of unmarked graves camps shelters
collateral damage of hospitals bombed—the reek

there is no news

that every dusk and dawn
you or your ancestors saw
is unique

look at that plume of plum quivering
on the horizon
before greying

as the night nurse
pulls on her uniform, her armpits stained
already with foreknowledge of strain

as the owls awaken, sun
-eyes scanning for rats and the city leopard
slinks from the disused drainpipe that's his lair

there is no news

of terraced hillsides glistening
33 thousand silvery reflections
each one shafted by blades
of 33 thousand rice seedlings as if
every moon echo is a buddha

walking on water, calm
except for that spurt of leaping carp
while below, ancient blood
-soaked land yields fertilizer for feuds
still singing in synapses lit

with quandom victories, each one of us a warrior
lost even to ourselves amidst

new histories discovered as the robot
does his rounds and satellites track
wars of every type while the planet's

thin skin flutters flags
of flame till smoke billows oblations to the pyres
of our unborn while the Arora Borealis pleats
the sky in jewel shades mined in the lava
fed underground womb, which rumbles

there's no news
that grace pours

no news
that night cleanses cities
so daybreak is fresh

no news
that love rises
to the stratosphere
like a loaf in an oven

there is no news
that Kairos is potential every moment
trembling
in your palms

Highway

Sampurna Chattarji

He points out all the shades of green—
hard dark for cauliflower,
soft light for jowar,
almost white on the aydusa tree,
almost lemon on the lemon.

Between bajra and jowar such tender gradations,
between brinjal and berry
none that I can see.

I am learning an entire landscape
crop by crop—
aydusa is the matchstick tree,
that's all its soft wood is good for,
divel makes the thick oil that keeps
bugs away from stocks of rice.

Faalsa, erinda.
Castor, cabbage.

Each pronounces the other's words wrong.
Yet our glee is congruent, contagious, warm.
There's nothing we wouldn't be willing to accept,
my blood—dark ignorance, his blood—deep knowing.

Chikoo green, guava green, eucalyptus
green with the mist of other terrains,
here, feel the milky green of its scent,

see the mango's green as function of taste,
not colour.

Somewhere along the way, when I say,
delighted to have spotted one familiar green
at last—the green-green of *isn't that grass?*
he doesn't laugh but says instead,
It is, that's the grass the cows will eat,
and so I tell him of my friend, the poet, her family
of grass-growers in Provence.

And then, I am silenced.

Such pride in his voice as he tells me—
Do you know, we wouldn't have reached so fast
if four thousand trees hadn't been cut!

Four thousand trees cut to build a highway.

Each unique symphony of green
stumped, felled, fallen,
killed without a thought.

Above the juicy-green grass
clouds of purple flowers float.

I will not ask him to name them for me now.

I need to list the greens before I lose them,
before I forget, I need to list the greens,
this teemingness of greens before
they die, flattened

from many-hued complexity
into monochromatic, hated
one.

Waggle Dance of the Bees

Nishi Chawla

Where the gauze footed foragers chant and disappear
Amid the burnished color, of clover and of meadow flowers?

Where the honeycombs ordered the gardens into bloom,
Setting out fearless, untamed, for the hatchet swings above.

Those burly roving machines made primroses nod, extract
Searching through, shod with a humming, feverish fanning.

Where velvet tones rang out, buccaneer rovers circulating
Over sunny gold, thread their busy wings over blue and yellow.

Those swarthy beings born, disciplined masonry machines
Threading their short stings dark in the light of the white daisy

Why do they not tempt anymore with their vagrant hum and glare
Sip rollicking, pastoral bandits, stooping over easy clovers?

Those summer afternoons boring holes, through the mouths
Of opened flowers, gather honey to dream within their bloodstream.

Whither their quiet toil, dipping, deploying their light pinnace
To light up the air, feed upon the wild flowers to burn, heedlessly?
That indefinite buzz, the will to chase, pollinate, tilt away,
Bewildered, consumed with a hidden quaff, the light takes a hint.

Where did they go, those hexagonal cells with honied hives,
Why does the summer sun no longer bring them alive, revive?

Dipping, climbing, swarming to the summit, skilfully spread
Wax and sing to vibrating honeycombs, waving antennae.

Whither those doomed colonies, busy bees lifting their
Painted thighs, to stare at the mocking skies. Serenade.

Death on the nip of dawn burns in the mountains, inlaid,
Teasing, evading, roaming, akin to their symphony.

Nest

Maxine Chernoff

'Always the quaking of relief.'—John Ashbery

In a swamp the mangroves shade the nest of eggs blue as
your eyes, who know the century's sorrow as light knows the drift
    of a feather through turbulent air.

You whose vows evaporate like mist from an ocean where starfish
        and algae feel
the touch of an invisible poison in water's slow retreat of grace,
        and blueness is reflection
of a steepled, latticed sky.

Trellised world, which pleads in low tones for a window where
        ledgers fill
with threads and feathers of birds, whose beaks crush certain
        berries in their ripeness, this small economy of need.

Colossal Wreck

Robert Coats

> 'Round the decay
> *Of that colossal Wreck, boundless and bare*
> *The lone and level sands stretch far away.*
> Ozymandias'
> Percy Bysshe Shelley, 1818

We thought our 'Shining City on the Hill'
would last forever.
With our missiles and megatons
no foe could defeat us,
certainly not a tiny microbe.

What a pleasure it was
to hop on a plane to Paris,
hear the engines roar,
feel their thrust pressing us
back into our deep seats.

And every year,
a new shiny 4X4 with knobby tires
and such a nice smell inside.
Gas was cheap, and what a thrill
to rip across the empty desert.

Then: fields of withered corn,
towns consumed in firestorms
or washed away.

In the lobby of the Miami Marriott,
the marble floor decorated
with barnacles and plastic flotsam.

I Want to Bring Back

Geraldine Connolly

My organdy Easter dress and straw hat
with a navy ribbon, tight green blossoms
in April, gravestones among apple trees,
the Virgin's long blue robe, the startled ringing
of the altar bell like breaking icicles, that moment
when bread changes into the body of God.

Bring back crocuses and Easter chicks, reborn Jesus,
dogwoods and sycamores, who wore their blazing hats
of color. Eggs and lilies, the first moment
the orchard above the farmhouse blossomed
pink above the muddy Pennsylvania creek, a ring
near furrowed fields, of laden apple trees,

pheasants with wings like helicopter blades, trees
that bloomed, lifting their faces toward God,
the whole of the newly ploughed garden bringing
        thoughts of hope. We tied on our hats
and to the ribbons fastened dry blossoms
with certainty, and that quiet instant

before we prayed became the moment
we wandered, lost among the trees,
muddied our stockings, crushed blossoms
beneath our shoes, cried out to the old God
to save us from falling. I remember that
once we were innocent, once we wore our ring

of belief like a badge, a feeling of being wrung
clean as we prayed, as if we could begin again.
I call to innocence, to girls in Communion hats
about to ascend the steep rows of church steps
to kneel, to bow and greet their god
as rows of widows and penitents like dark blossoms

light candles in the apse, their flame blossoms
illuminating the faithful, gathered and singing
songs of praise, hymns to the one God,
our faith restored, all of this in the moment
before mystery approached, belief failed, before trees
of new knowledge grew up into the heat
and fervor of the world. Tight green blossoms,
gravestones in the shade of apple trees, I call and
call to them. There is no answer

We Watch the Signs

Michael Cope

We watch the signs in numbness and regret.
Midwinter summer, chaos in the year,
And still our money's on the outside bet.

Why this unease? We know that some upset
Will switch our fortunes, now at full career.
We watch the signs in numbness and regret:

The hurricanes, the polar ice in sweat,
The rising heat, the changing atmosphere,
And still our money's on the outside bet . . .

Oh, if our stumbling nag would only get
A move on . . . But it won't. Let's have a beer
And watch the signs, in numbness and regret.

It isn't over till the end—oh but
It's over long before. Hopes disappear,
And still our money's on the outside bet.

By now they've reached the final straight, and yet
We look away, while at the edges, clear,
We note the signs in numbness and regret.
And still our money's on the outside bet.

Audubon

Alfred Corn

Early America's gone, extinct like the passenger
Pigeon, skies once an avalanche of migration
Now vacant but for clouds and vapor trails, the rare
Arrowhead of bleating Canada geese or loner hawk.
And the land below laid bare, its forests cut and bartered,
Exchanged for tarmac, strip malls and gated suburbs.

When ancestors at seven removes paused to scan
The wild, impassable except where pierced
By trails non-natives couldn't scout, they guessed
More than was sayable about the unsurveyable,
Their own intrusion trivial. Audubon differed.
Subduing the awe reconnaissance offered him,
He leaned on his rifle atop the abrupt promontory,
And indreamed a misted river valley symphonic
With piped solfège from the birds of America.

Brushstrokes of oil or wash won their idea.
Taut silk blades extended a fan to grasp buffeting
Updrafts, a shot taken on the wing, one gape-staring
Fish cramponed in airborne rapture, nature's tandem
Food chain kidnapped and shipped to the Royal Society.

What couldn't travel was context—limitless terraces
Of air, the woodlands slip-knotted with vine and briar,
Creeks sweet with tannin, the crossfire gaze of bear and cougar,
Scats, a ribcage stripped by crook-necked scavengers,
Insurgence of mosquito tribes, ponds paved with lilies,

A singular glycerine bead distilled on each veined disc.
Epochs that saw the uprush of aeronautic tribes
Filmed in mirroring water-color are passed and gone.
A wilderness, a fauna, erased. Not banished, vanished.
It won't return, or not until the looters go. Passengers.

The Story Queen

Henry Crawford

Sick of sticking needles in her arm
she turned to stories. Kept them in a purse.
There was the one about an invisible horse
who came to the windows of children at night.
She had one about a right-brained tax accountant
who made an enemy of a left-brained sushi chef.
She wrote them on the BART, going into Oakland.
There was the story of a leaf-consoling oak tree.
And Beowulf reimagined as a spaghetti western.
She did her makeup on the train. Praying into her
lipstick case. There was a story of twin parallel lines
fated never to meet. A mountain that could feel
its own weight and a mosquito who knew it was alive.
She worked making calls in a windowless call center.
There was a story that never got off the ground
and one that ended up in the clouds. A boy who proved
his love by tumbling all night in a laundromat dryer.
She walked beside the Bay at lunch. Gray and moody.
There was the story of a missed bar mitzvah
and one about a telephone call at the end of a long
divorce. There was the night that never came
and the day that never followed it. She had
moths in a time of light, bats in an age of dark
and a worm who appeared before Alfred the Great.
She came home to a high-rise and a half-loved cat.
Hung her purse on a hook by the door. Labored
under the spell of a magnanimous grace
most of us will never experience.

Whale Shark

Mamang Dai

1.   *Whale shark*

Trust is a gift
even though a brutal blow
may end your life
trust is a gift, but
Whale shark
never let us know where you go.

Trust is the gift
that sways you in the deep
moving close to men and boats
gulping light and water
big as an island
your breath parts the waters

A vision of rare beauty
if you survive this encounter
the frenzy of saviours, scientists, do-gooders
even entranced, awe struck me
Whale shark, never yield your secrets,
slide away, plummet down
to your secret continents,
never let us know where you go.

Dump

Mustansir Dalvi

Can't turn away from the smell,
can you? Nor avert your gaze
from the United Colours
of wet, putrefying waste?

Petition editors, signature campaigners
accumulate evidence in the betweens
of a city going to dogs, as assiduously
as a refuse bin repels garbage.

Each sense organ appropriates
a part of the cogitation after
every mess you cannot
but step into. Each house-gully

is re-envisioned full fifty times digitally
and you spend twenty-five nights
photoshopping its pungent tinctures
to satisfaction. Take the smells to bed.

May your dreams make vivid the reek
of your sleeping body. Make it mumble
the secret parseltongue of your own stench
brought home from waking life.

Your only fulfillment is in
the fetishism of throbbing thrash.

Of Ledges and Moss

Keki Daruwalla

You don't have to notice a gun
to visualize black buck falling
in a fusillade of hoofs.

And the bellies of wild geese
flying in formation?
What is there to visualize
I hear a gunshot
though I don't see a gun.
I don't even hear the shot—
It's all in the mind.
It will spin as it falls
huddling into its wings.

Just because I haven't
pulled out a pad of moss
from some rocky ledge,
doesn't mean I do not hear
the rip and tear of rending.
Just because I do not shoot
quail or partridge it doesn't mean
this birdlessness travelling towards me
like a visible void,
does not smother me.
Nature's empire is not confined
to forest and savannah.
The soul is also one of its habitats

Animal Planet*

Ranajit Das

'I am the master of this universe, my fun and frolic are the only things that matter, besides which there is no other truth or mystery, in this creation'—Whenever the modern man thinks like this, he turns into a beetle. A stout, strong black beetle of the Amazon basin. He roams the branches of the rubber trees with a snobbish swagger. He sits in a coffee house of Rio de Janeiro, wearing spectacles and a grave expression on his face, indulging in intellectual discourse about musk and Michel Foucault. In fact, that coffee house is nothing but a tall branch of a huge rubber tree, under which flows the river Amazon. And in the water of that river swims a 'water-monkey' fish. The fish has two long beards on its chin. Amid the dense rainforest, suddenly the 'water-monkey' jumps from the water up to a height of six feet in the air, neatly gobbles up the beetle, and disappears under the waters of the Amazon.

---

* Translated from the Bengali by Nirmal Kanti Bhattacharjee

Almanac of Faithful Negotiations

Todd Fleming Davis

> *'Here, at the edge of heaven,*
> *I inhabit my absence.'*
> —Tu Fu

On the first day, we find evidence of elk but not the elk themselves.

On the second, we see the charred and blackened sleeves fire
leaves but not a single flame.

By the third day, the oldest trees have already ascended but the
microbial mouths buried in the dirt remain.

After four days, our minds flood with rivers and creeks, and we
find it hard to speak, except in mud and stone.

On the fifth, ravens decorate a white-oak snag, croaking in the
voices of our drunk uncles, reminding us whose house we live in.

Six days gone, a fisher stands on hind legs, stares across the
meadow's expanse, dares us to approach the porcupine-
corpse, muzzle red with the body's sugar.

When the last day comes, only minutes before dawn, susurration
of wind, stars moving back into the invisible, all of us
wondering when we will join them.

Takamatsu: Ritsurin Garden*

Lucille Lang Day

Grafted together, black and red pine embrace—The Happy Couple of Ritsurin Garden, where six ponds brim with koi, yellow or mottled orange and white. Thirteen hills, one called 'Mt. Fuji,' surround a man-made waterfall and teahouses in a landscape of oak, pine, plum, and cherry trees holding out tufts of needles or leaves at the ends of artfully gnarled limbs; boulders in strict arrangements; shrubs trimmed into balls and domes. The garden took more than 100 years to complete—more than enough time for formation of a vortex of floating plastic pellets that albatrosses mistake for fish eggs and feed to chicks who die of starvation, while speckled koi nibble algae in the ponds, and scraps of discarded bottles and bags gather in the sea.

---

* Honorable Mention, Prose Poem Category, Soul-Making Keats Literary Competition. First published in *Nostos: Poetry, Fiction, and Art*.

Wild, Wild

Barry Dempster

Wild, how trees claw at one another,
rocks buried half-alive, spiders spitting
mid-air. We are not to confuse these wilds
with human pathology. Nor to let literature
weep pathetic. Wild is numb, is brainless.
Where nothing ever happens twice.

This tree is a wooden cell; it knocks
in the wind and grows. This rock is a mineral
deposit. And the spider, the most alive
we'd say (like us), is a dark enzyme
oozing in the so-called light. A man may walk
through these wilds, or he may not.
If a poet, he will probably want to tell:
the same weeping willow again and again.

Numb is somehow tender to the touch—moss,
bark, breeze. A beautiful brainless rock,
the act of sitting an act of love.
Each soft spider dashing the wrist
brings one thrill of skin alive.

Wild, how trees touch back, rocks
muscle into open hands, spiders land.
A man sits confused in the forest,
pathetically talking to himself.
Everything feels and can't forget.

All men are pathological. Weeping,
they bring the adjectives down.
Always another man, half-awake, dangling
in the air. This is man's makeup,
the literature of all kinds.
The same man tough as trees, deep
as rock, spitting dreams. Wild,
he says. Wild.

Unburying the Bird

Toi Derricotte

Buried birds
are usually
dead.
Fallen from the sky
because of too much
something.
    Too much high.
    Too much steep.
    Too much long.
    Too much deep.
But sometimes
one has been known
to go underground.
You do not hear a peep
for years.
Then one day,
you go back to the spot
thinking you will not find
a feather or a few
scattered bones
and you hear something
pecking trying
to get out of there.
You are afraid to believe
it is still alive.
Afraid that even if it is
in being freed, it will die.
Still,

slowly,
you go about freeing the bird.
You scrape away the grave
which in some mysterious way
has not suffocated her.
You free her scrawny head.
Her dangling wing.
You keep thinking her body
must be broken beyond healing.
You keep thinking the delicate
instruments of flight
will never pull again.
Still,
you free her.
Feed her from the tip of your finger.
Teach her the cup of your hand.
You breathe on her.
One day,
you open up your hand
and show her sky.

The Road Home

Hemang Desai

Taking the road home, not recently taken,
Has it ever happened that you went on,
Then, looked around and behind to see
You'd lost way, probably, one May day,
From simple blanking or sudden memory loss,
—Transient global amnesia, as they say—
Lush green memory, seventy years strong,
Densely packed, ten thousand at a stretch,
Put to axe since the highway is to be six-laned
To give motorists seamless travel experience?

While stepping on the gas
Over a road freshly laid, did you ever feel
The tar throbbed, leapt and clung to your feet,
Like the memory, three centuries deep,
Of a poet who, hauled out of his tomb,
Left with thorns in his chest?*

As these deadly roads now,
The running scabs over sore earth,
Lie deserted like black desert,
Fit only for a crowned bug's prowl,
Have you, holed up with your grains stockpile,
Finally thought about the memory

---

* From *Dar-Firaaq-e-Gujarat* (On separation from Gujarat), a poem by 17th century Urdu poet Wali-Gujarati whose tomb in Ahmedabad was razed in 2002.

The six *musahara* kids, not very far,
Bent over patches of bentgrass,
—As even rats have made themselves scarce—
Relive every day, a memory old as millennia,
The size of the universe, and
Your ride on the road to amnesia?

If you did, you already know,
It's time to turn around, bro.

If

Imtiaz Dharker

If we could pray. If
we could say we have come here
together, to grow into a tree,
if we could see our blue hands
holding up the moon, and hear
how small the sound is
when it slips through
our fingers into water,
when the meaning of words melts
away and sugarcane speaks
in fields more clearly
than our tongues,
when a child takes
a stick as long as itself

and rolls a wheel
down a lane on wings of dust,
in control, would we
think then that we should thank
someone? If we knew
we could turn, and turning
feel that things could be different.
But we are unused
to gratitude, if we could lose
our pride, bend down
look for peace on the iron
ground. If we could

kneel.

Ants: Red and Black*

Hemant Divate

Ants whisper to each other
about work constantly.
Perhaps they warn each other about a foot-wide ocean up ahead,
or about an inch and a half high hill they have to traverse,
or about the stupid trick played on them by a cruel man
spilling salt across their path.

Ants hold a grudge against these giant, hideous humans
because they have decreed that only red ants are to be killed
while showering their grace upon the black ones.
They seem to practice racism on ants as well.
We red ants are not without mercy,
when do we ever bite sleeping babies?
In fact, only when someone intrudes into our anthills
do we ever lose our heads?

Humans are unaware how crafty those black ants can be—
should anyone cross their path, they crawl into their ears
and tickle them endlessly, and they can leave
those who threaten them completely beyond help.

It's only men who hide their faces
unable to say anything when faced with adversity.

---

* Translated from the Marathi by Mustansir Dalvi

The Believers in Mercy*

Sharon Dolin

This is how Noah must have felt:
go to sleep, rain. wake up, rain.
the wooden flaps on the cabin leaking
inside.

This is how the world often ends

the animals getting restive—too busy huddling
in the cold wet wind to mate or eat.

No one thinks about the cries of the
thousand thousand creatures who floated on
branches, the left-over pieces of houses

those others who cursed Noah and his family,
suffocating on water, paddled off
into history's amnesia.

They were the best of carpenters, they the gatherers of
     pomegranates
now floating on the surface
of rivers, they the trappers of birds—whose wet feathers made
     them too heavy to fly and an easy catch,
though no fire will take—they the believers in mercy.

Surely the rain will stop before everyone drowns

---

* From *Heart Work,* The Sheep Meadow Press, 1995

and the crops are all smothered. Before the grain
all rots in its storage sacks
carried to higher and ever higher ground.

Being descended from Noah, I should side
with his story.

But there must have been some deserving
of forgiveness: women craving
someone else's man, the petty gamblers,
the avaricious husbands, the envious children.

Outside, save for the chosen pair:
the field mice squeal all night in the rain

raccoons knit their claws in prayer and
finally live peaceably together, the groundhog is rained
out of his hole.

A Picnic

Ian Duhig

At first almost nothing,
an inkling of porcelain
as of a wind-chime's:
then, breakers crash—

windows web and give
splintering rainbows,
sockets fizz and pop,
shelves pour books.

Outside, lawns slump,
drunk, and are gone,
apple trees thrown
like brides' bouquets.

The cliff races inland
tearing down fields,
fences, cows, streets,
pillows of rainclouds.

Suddenly its huge roar
is drowned by silence,
the world films itself
with slow motion grace.

Clothes don't flap
now: fathoming,

dance arm in arm
with no wallflowers.

The tablecloth trick
reverses in thick air
settling for a picnic
in the kelp forest.

A saucer see-saws
down this way, that,
to catch the teacup
gathering this storm.

Viaduct Greene

David Ebenbach

That's what it takes: a subway dies and you make it
a garden. Even underground, even in the uncreated
dark. There, where the sweat of this city is hardened
into its stalactites. Cement, too, is stone, though not
under these our hands; we light this expanse of
soda bottles and human waste and see the verdant
potential. Someday—it's true—someday we'll walk
below the street, not afraid of broken glass or needles.
We'll stay on the groomed paths, hands held, a date,
overhead the underside and also a lamp-post that
brings back the era of gaslight—ivy across the fresh
brick—and wonder at what comes from destruction.
Which is us.

Scene of a Dismantled Village outside Pripyat

Meg Eden

What will be done with all these dishes
now that we're dead? The trees
have no need for silverware.
Think of what our mothers would say,
seeing our heirloom china,
covering the forest floor!

The forest has become
a radioactive living room.
Debris makes a tablecloth,
the corrugated roofs placemats.
But who dines here now besides the deer?

Inside one cup, a chipmunk
makes its home. Inside another,
a spider breeds. Soon, her eggs
will hatch and from where
there was one body, there will be
thousands. Think about that—
something still lives after all of this.

Seagull Lullaby

Mohsen Emadi

'Authorities lose track of thousands of unaccompanied child refugees each year.'

—Deutsche Welle, 2019*

11.23 a.m. sharp in Helsinki.
Language has vertigo for 10 minutes
and immediately finds himself on a bus
heading in the direction of geographical north.
The fact the bus driver checked his tickets
and put him on seat no. 13
has yet to be made clear.
On 71 seats of the bus
70 passengers are sitting
all are different versions of a person
and each could be described with 70 different verbs:
the one who laughs, the one who cries, the one who signs,
        etcetera.
With a simple look in the mirror of the bus
language understands that such a situation
has nothing to do with the metaphor of the road and the
        passengers:
no story will be told
and on the other hand all the stories shall fall verb by verb.
in the first station, near midnight, somewhere near a harbor
all the passengers get out

---

* https://www.dw.com/en/germanys-thousands-of-missing-refugee-minors/a-47270354

and the wind with all its transformations
lashes the body of language.
Language mourns
using the throats of seagulls.

2

11.23 a.m. sharp in Helsinki
is not a metaphor
however it can determine the place and time of a death or a birth
or inform one about a return or a departure.
What remains clear is the door of a car opening
someone getting out
and meanwhile he doesn't get on the bus that goes toward
    geographical north
and language falls because of vertigo.
The intense cold of the harbor, the empty streets and the harsh
    winds
prevent us from foregrounding the vertigo of language
each poem caused a situation like this for language
in addition at 11:23 a.m. in Helsinki
nothing is poetical
especially now
in this corner of the harbor
where a strong rain is forecast
and the rain-pregnant clouds are massing under the shirt of
    language.
before lightning
before rain
before language gets in the crew-less, traveler-less ship
it must be clear who was in the bus with language
and why he is avoiding any metaphor.

3

At 11.23 a.m. sharp in Helsinki
in those ten mysterious minutes
the memory of language faces some possible incidents:
Ten minutes where a man looks into the ocean in the eyes of a
     woman
to discover he is lost forever
ten minutes where the first kiss occurs
ten minutes where a bridge falls down
ten minutes where blood leaves a body
ten minutes where the nest of seagulls slips off
the slope of the rooftop on the other side of the window
and reaches the surface of the street
but no matter how much the memory of language
gets manipulated by poetry
it cannot give a clear image of the incidents
without those seventy verbs that got off the bus in the harbor
it's not even clear that the wind, the lashes, the cloud and the
     wind
or this harbor
belong to a historical or poetical determinism.
The harbor in the movements of the crew-less, traveler-less ship
is far from sight
in all thousand cabins of the ship the voice of a child is heard
the cold caress of the wind resembles a sad lullaby
'the heart of the mother with the child and the heart of the child
     with the wolf of the sea'
The tides of this ocean
are not related to the moon
they refer to a thousand homeless children

that stand each time on the deck of the ship
and one by one are thrown into the sea.

4

At 11.23 a.m. sharp in Helsinki
language faces its incapacities
faces a man
that gets out of the car or does not
in a street that exists or does not
to reach a bus, a harbor, a ship or not
whether on earth or on water
in the distance between one door and another
that gets opened and gets closed.
Those mysterious ten minutes
form a Moebius strip
that coincidentally juxtaposes the before and the after
and the depth of the ocean and its surface.
As long as this ship advances on
broken embraces
or that car on unfinished kisses,
a man and a woman
are still walking on a forest road
arm in arm
and always stop under a specific tree
both are aborted embryos kept in a wooden box
where fire burns
in the far away
the wind of the ocean takes lost verbs
to all shores.

5*

In a small room in Helsinki
with a window facing the inclined rooftop of a house
and the lost nests of the seagulls on it
the eyes of a man a woman
lose the ancient function of seeing
the verb 'to see' is handed to the skin
to look into the pores of darkness
with the two thousand eyes of a thousand drowned kids,
the bone sees the bone
and the blood listens
the tick tock of a clock
at 11.23 a.m. sharp in Helsinki
language was getting out of the car
to meet with his past
with a forgotten lullaby
that lips sing to the ear
on both sides of the ocean.
Say it you let it rain!

---

* Translated from the Persian by Lyn Coffin

Drought on the Navajo Reservation*

Gail Entrekin

Three roan mares showed up outside our trailer
heads down, ribs protruding like carcasses, and
while we watched from the doorway, they slumped
down, one leg at a time, two of them dead
by the time they hit the ground. We went out
with a bucket of water, Lincoln and me, and
we set it down by the last mare standing and
she let us come, had come to us, we figured,
where they never come, like they were almost
spirits and had to trust us now, and she slowly
moved her head and drank. Ten gallons a day
they need, and there hasn't been but a drop or two
in 15 years, the ground like rock, cracked, the soil
snatched away into the air, nothing green to eat
and not even much that's brown, and still we live here,
hauling water for coins from the watering station.
No one on the res that hasn't seen them dead,
3,00,000 of them sharing 27,000 square miles of pitiless land
where we used to see them blow out like the wind, their manes
whipping, their fine legs pounding. They've got to forage
32 pounds a day, and now their mouths are full of mud, so weak
they stick in at the watering hole and they just lie down
and die.
These sacred horses were here before the People came.
We go out every day to meet them, we bring our wagon,
fill the old, deserted troughs, and they come right to us,

* Previously published in *Wild: Marin Poetry Center Anthology, 2019*

their big eyes full of dust and flies hovering,
and they don't understand what it is
that's happening to them
to all of us.
They just drink.

Your Forest

Annie Finch

Your forest goes as green as love.
Your ferns are dappled near the ground,
and moss they dapple curls above
stones that your glacier dappled down.

Your night is sadness well-contained
within the sap that runs the stem
of plants that grow along the night
and root at morning. Joy finds them,

while oceans, vast because they are lost
(like ruined roads left on the land)
take your kind waters home each time
that they, pushing raptly at the sand,

make tides with your evaporate rain.
The ocean is at peace again.

Far algae grows, the blue stays smooth,
and in dim light, the beach is soothed.

Your forest grows as green as love,
your night is sadness well-contained,
and oceans, lost because they are vast,
make tides with your evaporate rain.

An Awful Climate*

Maria Galina

Our climate is so awful
that all the peripatetics
sink to the bottom of an endless black winter
before they can agree
on anything useful
Our climate is so awful
that the ever coughing Diogenes
has relocated from his dank container
under the elevated heating main
and into the fields of blooming asphodels
Our climate is so awful
that Dante and Beatrice left
after their first conjugal night
for a honeymoon in Thailand
but have never come back
living there happily ever after
and never dropping us a line
Our climate is so awful
that cynocephalic cyclopes
have migrated from the fringes of the world
to our industrial landfills
they talk like us walk like us
and are in no way different from us now

---

* Translated from the Russian by Philip Nikolayev

From Petrarch at Mount Ventoux

Kevin Gallagher

Number 188

O sun, we both marvel at the same branch,
which I wish was pointing at me. I reach

out my finger to touch her sweet peace.
She has no equal since Adam's curse.

Let us stay and glow as we gaze at her
before you slip away into the dark:

taking out the day, covering the hills,
taking my love with you and away from me.

Your shadow rolls down the sloping hill,
turns to a blanket, then covers my light

where my magnificent little laurel lies.
You stretch toward my face and cover my eyes.

That sapling you come from, here in my heart.
I can no longer see that blessed place.

Last Serenity*

Antonio Gamoneda

You hardly hear the destruction of the wood,
the blind termites in their veins.
You dream of needles and cupboards
full of shade.

This could be your final nap.
How much childhood under the eyelids.

Like a clumsy horsefly in the summer,
you remove your mother's cold serge from your face.
You have not suspected in vain.
Your serenity is excessive. You go
to wake up in oblivion.

The twilight has settled on my hands.
It has come through the sick laurel.
I don't want to think, or be loved, or be happy, or remember,
I just want to feel this light in my hands,
and ignore all the faces,
and that the birds pass before my eyes
and I do not know that they are gone.

I see cracks and shadows on white walls.
Soon there will be more cracks and more shadows,
and later there will be no white walls.

---

* *Translated from the Spanish by Nishi Chawla*

It is old age, it flows in my veins like water pierced by moans.
All questions are going to stop.
The late sun has settled on my hands and they come to me,
confused in a single substance,
the thought and its disappearance.
It is the ultimate serenity.
Nobody waits for me or knocks on my door.
All signs are empty.
My only learning is forgetting.

Forest

Forrest Gander

Erogenous zones in oaks
slung with
stoles of lace-lichen the

sun's rays spilling

through leaves in
broken packets a force

call it night-time

thrusts mushrooms up
from their lair

of spawn mycelial

loam the whiff of port
they pop into un-

trammelled air with the sort of
gasp that follows
a fine chess move

like memories are they? or punctuation? was it
something the earth said
to provoke our response

tasking us to recall

an evolutionary

course our long ago

initiation into
the one-
among-others

and within

my new-born noticing have you
popped up beside me love

or were you here from the start

a swarm of meaning and decay

still gripping the underworld

both of us half-buried holding fast
if briefly to a swelling

vastness while our coupling begins

to register in the already

awake compendium that offers

to take us in you take me in

and abundance floods us floats
us out we fill each
with the other all morning

breaks as birdsong over us

who rise to the surface

so our faces might be sprung

Sanctum

Dawn Garisch

In early morning, I escape up our mountain—
the dark island rising out of a turbulent sea
of city lights, fumes and sounds. The path calls
me away from all our human busyness to where

time stills to a trickle through algae. Here,
where the shadow of an owl swooping from a tree
is the central necessity, I drink living water
and find a slower way to breathe. Pausing

in a brush of fynbos, I see the sky catch alight—
clouds are burning in the dawn's first rays
above the scattered coals of streetlight.
There's no escape. I must descend into the day

but with the scent of buchu on my hands,
and, in the sanctum of my eye, the fleeting flare of owl.

To Nature - Three Sonnets

Rainer Maria Gassen

I

What garden did you dream of planting, when
the season was in throng; what seedling did
you favour and what was the promise, what
the chore to help the weakling fighting through;
waking would have deeply gashed your flesh, too
brittle to be bleeding, yet all brimming
with your life to recreate, to fend off
who might dare you to accept his bidding;
the challenge is all yours, the power and
the stratagem, as time can't mean a thing,
so long as you don't need to count the years
by what is left of glory and defeat;
this your land, you might be big in, calls you
to think on, whether Autumn's name were Spring.

II

Your shoulders carry weights of centuries,
of generations' individuals,
of lands unknown and foreign languages,
experience of your own inspiration;
if I kissed your neck, took in the flavours
silently distilled in thorny depths of
your enthralling frame, would I partake of them,
or should you try me for my trespass, speak
out loud and point your dagger at my guilt;
hide from me, and send me searching, I will
roam forsaken territories, drink from

brackish waters, lose my compass, swim through
quicksand, find myself spat out by your heavy
gales, wake up to feel my quivering lips aflame.

III

The rains fall colder now; the steady sheen
off slanting roofs is dirty grey from clouds
    deliberately turning darker shades
    of white, the vestiges of autumn noon;
    yours alone is this bewitching hour
    full of guile yet potent remedy in
your fulfilling hands, so give me my full
measure rubbing light onto my closing lids;
    I realize I was fair game to you,
    yet never once could I be tempted to
walk out on you, much less so, when your spells
were slowly wearing off or wholly spent;
    should this poem fail to win you over
there'll be hundreds if not thousands more of them.

Picking Peaches*

Christine Gelineau

Even before we're close enough
to reach to them we smell
the sweet offertory of their ripening.

Birds lift with loud reluctance
leaving behind opened suns
of soft-fleshed fruit.

He steadies the ladder
while I rise among the leaves
handing down the warm-skinned globes.

Peach by peach they drop
from my fingers to the cradle
of his outstretched hands

and for that moment we
too are as filled to the skin
as fruit.

---

* 'Picking Peaches' appeared in *Remorseless Loyalty* (Ashland, OH: Ashland
  Poetry Press /Ashland University, 2006)

How Does an 'Un' Get Added to Our Ease?*

P. N. Gopikrishnan

Why is it that ants don't draw men along
like they carry a dead cockroach?

Why don't parrots carry men
in their beaks like cornstalks?

Why is it that no goat ever eats men,
but only chews green leaves?

Reasons are very small,
but we think they are big

What we call a tree is also
the mark of a vanished forest

What we call cat is what was left
after the exodus of beasts

A pool is also a drop that fell
as the wild stream fled the land

All our freedoms carry
the marks of aggression.

Beneath the goodness of a Gandhi or a Buddha

---

* Translated from the Malayalam by K. Satchidanandan

lies the shadow of an undeclared war.

The lane of thought that
Karl Marx went down to walk is also
a zigzag passage along which
a snake had slithered away

The rooster Socrates said he owed
to the Roman god is one
that had dropped down
from a flock of birds

Reasons are small,
small, extremely small.

Plants are studying us
like we study them.

As we turn the small into big
with our microscopes,
they are also turning us small
with another lens.

Letter To My Great, Great Grandchild
after Matthew Olzmann

J.P. Grasser

Oh button, don't go thinking we loved pianos
more than elephants, air conditioning more than air.

We loved honey, just loved it, and went into stores
to smell the sweet perfume of unworn leather shoes.

Did you know, on the coast of Africa, the Sea Rose
and Carpenter Bee used to depend on each other?

The petals only opened for the Middle C their wings
beat, so in the end, we protested with tuning forks.

You must think we hated the stars, the empty ladles,
because they conjured thirst. We didn't. We thanked

them and called them lucky, we even bought the rights
and named them for our sweethearts. Believe it or not,

most people kept plants like pets, and hired kids
like you to water them, whenever they went away.

And ice! Can you imagine? We put it in our coffee
and dumped it out at traffic lights, when it plugged up

our drinking straws. I had a dog once, a real dog,
who ate venison and golden yams from a plastic dish.

He was stubborn, but I taught him to dance and play
dead with a bucket full of chicken livers. And we danced

too, you know, at weddings and wakes, in basements
and churches, even when the war was on. Our cars

we mostly named for animals, and sometimes we drove
just to drive, to clear our heads of everything but wind.

A Forest Track

Hywel Griffiths

With a four-wheel drumroll
the spring sunrise
casts its spell
until the day
steals the trees
to the chainsaw's blade.

For the New Millennium

Adalet Barış Günersel

A place
where laughter is a habit
 and not something that occurs once in a while,
where tears are for happiness
 and not for an invisible knife in our bosoms,
where deep sighs are for a lover
 and not for a starving child,
where running is for joy
 and not to escape,
where guns are no means
 instead of all means,
where the media give us inspiration
 and not examples of violence,
where dreams turn into reality
 and do not remain imaginary,
where opportunities are equal
 as well as people,
where bleeding is minimized
 and loving maximized,
where the only blindness is to sex, color and race
 and not to the world,
where no superiors or inferiors exist,
 where seeing is not prevented by belief,
where justice is just
 and not simply a word,
where mother nature is taken care of
 and not raped,
where father time is enjoyed

and not wasted,
where 'God' gives relief
     and not excuses for discrimination,
where the sun shines through our eyes
     and music is composed by our souls,
where the oceans' clean blue calms our minds
     and the depth deepens our hearts,
where life is lying in a field of buttercups
     and not striving to breathe.

This could be our world
in the third millennium
     —there's nothing we can't achieve.

The End's Nigh

Kimiko Hahn

When winter is warm as spring,
I know polar bears and shrimp alike
die from the high temps. I know
we're conveyed this warning
because local flora are not
the sole harbingers of ruin;
because even fungus offers insight
(our islands are all connected).
I look out my cooperative window
and know that pink and red buds
on the highest branches do not signal
an early gift of colour nor early demise
of influenza. It hurts the soul,
this radiant January day
that incites what we admit
is wrong. Yes, even sightings
of the migratory birds en route
to land in the nearby lake.
They never leave. They know
the reeds and grasses, though not high,
though bereft of a green scent,
are here to stay. They know
in their migratory soul
to stay where food is plentiful,
in nature or overflowing
trash cans. The birds have insight
on survival without depending
on wing muscle. Their very

avian skeleton knows
not to bother flying.
The message to stay is sent
in the wind's transparent scent.
I am the owner of this warmth.
Not the sole owner. But at least
I confess while basking in the sight
of Canadian geese wintering
in this bland northern climate.
And crocus, daffodils, snow drops,
primrose, forsythia, hyacinths—
even dandelions along a highway—
once vernal signs,
now nature's prescient unease.
Doesn't the wind also have a soul?
The guy in the subway is shouting,

The end's in sight. Yes—high time to find no solace
in the sunshine. Algae in bloom is a sentence.

In the Absence of Man

Anna Halberstadt

Wild boars and porcupines
are roaming the forests of Galilee
Nature rejoices.
A man in his apartment in Kew Gardens
saw a family of raccoons
under his balcony
that he only knew
existed
but were never seen in Queens.

A sheep escaped her flock
in Portugal and grew
sixty pounds of fur
grazing in the mountains.
Journalists reported
that wolves had tried to eat her
but their teeth
could not penetrate
the fur.
This fluffy goofball posed for pictures.

The sky is abnormally blue over Broadway
as I am crossing Greene Street
white puffy clouds are
like clouds of gauze
in wards of COVID hospitals
with patients on oxygen
clinging to what is meant

for each one
as the remainder of his or her life.

Three Moirae are weaving overtime,
entangled in more threads
than they've ever handled.
Atropos can't manage
cutting them alone.
They have no time to wipe
their foreheads,
take a sip of water;
sweaty and exhausted,
like ICU doctors.

Manichaean

Richard Harteis

We went from rug rats to
Pre-pubescent farm kids.
Raw, but not particularly
Evil—like the tribe of boys
In Lord of the Flies who
cried when they killed Piggy
And staged a piggy ceremony
Not knowing what else to do.
Once my cousins stuck a straw
Up a frog's ass, blew him up
And set him putt putt putting
Across the pond's surface like
A little green motor boat.
If you nicked off the tail of a
Firefly and stuck it on your
Ring finger, it glowed
Phosphorescent for a
Long time, something to do.
Kids, nasty yes, but not
Really to blame. We planted
Adult seeds, and spent the
Rest of our lives trying to
Outlive what grew inside us.

More Sky Please

John Hennessy

More sky please push open the apartment shutters
crowbar the paint factory's broken window frames rip
tarpaper from the caving roof push it back crack it open

blast an airshaft through the neighbouring buildings snap
it back expose the bird-ridden drafts the wren's been busy
here mornings year round churr and chip golden open-throat

yodel smack in the sleep cycle soldered to feeder suet
in ivy like titmouse chickadee refusing to shift it back
Carolina Canada climate haywire more sky please rik tik tik

break open more light all the way past oil tank farms
creosote docks the Kill Van Kull slide by kingfisher flap
past cormorant incongruous flights parallel and merging

plunge into slap out of tidal pools the Fresh Kills beak
full of killifish and silversides crayfish and krill tarp
past the saltgrass and bridges fly Pulaski Skyway

Bayonne's silver buildings blank tower-blocks sky
wide as the river-mouth more sky more please push it back
past tankers and tugboats the last hulking cruise ship

lasers fired across a spinning disco ball wobble bass
and echo chamber dancing on deck past clanging buoys
waveless channels to deepest basin all things even

terns drop away sea and sky opened wide and empty

Gripping the Rests

W. N. Herbert

Remember that flight from Beijing to Paris
when, as the drinks were being served,
everything arose over the Gobi as though
held in a globe by the hands of angels:
glass, alcohol, stomach, heart—suspended
longer than the second of our denial.

After, as the captain so brightly explained
how very tensile our wings were, remember
how we still gripped the armchair rests, despite
having observed that this capacity of the hand,
although unique to our species, could not prevent
the plummeting of the plane.

It is surely in search of this grip that my hands slide
through each other, as, washing, I consider
the epidemiologist's remark: 'You always forget the thumbs.'
We measure our miasma with a song,
mouthing most unhappy birthdays—to our masters,
perhaps, or to that jester, Pilate.

So, amid both catastrophe and, worse,
good fortune's lull, the soul clenches, since
to unlock the once is to admit that tiny prophecy:
we are out of our depth, dexterity, and luck.
Our hands may flap together in an imprecation
which is also, uniquely, ours, but it shall not fly.

The Salt Lick

Scott Hightower

Now a large tumultuous family
that is more village than country
rents the house. I now am the landlord
of the landscape of my childhood.
Last one standing. The tontine is mine.
Not without pretenders and dispute.

A ways from the main gate, in front
of the house, off to the side of the approach
road, just as one comes up the hill
where the wild bronze turkeys
like to patrol, especially on rainy days,

near the antique oak with snake-like limbs
that drop to the ground—and curl back up
in search of Laocoön and his sons,
is the site of the ancient salt lick;
even less assuming than the old
rock reservoir, the weathered barn,
the house tucked among ancient oaks.

Even before my family became its stewards,
the common practice was to put out
salt to supplement (the natural supply long
depleted) for the wildlife and livestock.
Eventually, we built a water trough.
'Come, eat. Come, drink.'

In the light of each morning, and then
throughout the day, the cows amble up
and drink their bellies full. Their muzzles
drip with slobber, the green of grass
and moss, and water. Dark turkeys

sometimes approach when the cattle
are not there. Late at night, the varmints
come and drink. If it is a dark
night, their eyes betray
them. If it is a bright star-lit night,

their silhouettes portray
them. And in the hours
between night and morning,
the deer come, lick salt, and drink.

The Swamp Swallows Everything

Geoffrey Himes

The swamp swallows everything, nutritious and noxious alike.
Leaves and twigs fall from trees overhead,
lie on the water a while, then slowly sink,
changing from solid to liquid in slow motion,
even as the still water thickens into sludge.

When a boater tosses a soda can overboard
and discharges gasoline from the motor,
the swamp ingests that too.
The can will rust and bleed its colors
as it tilts and drops from sight.
The gas spreads across the bog like a flattened rainbow,
beautiful like so many poisons, and finally thins to nothing.

We too are swamps, jellied blood and organs in a thin skin sack.
We too swallow the tasty and the toxic,
sweet peaches and spoiled beef, kind words and bitter insults,
digesting it all into a soup of decay, slowly moving
toward the liquification beneath

Signs and Wonders

Paul Hoover

'If it is consistent, it is incomplete; if complete, inconsistent.'
—Kurt Gödel

For it will come to pass
that they live in Bakersfield
and the gardens of Coalinga,
where they enter the rock

and live in the rock
and remain in the rock when they die.
For their high-definition eyes
are more than nature and art,

and the dust of their seeing
paints them from within.
For they please themselves with images
and images of images,

Their lips are stung by bees;
their breasts yield no milk.
The miser lies down with the master,
the skinny clerk with the fat.

For the land of plenty
is the land of baristas.
For their sisters work at Walmart,
and their unions are non-existent.

They prepare the table with Popeye's;
fuel desire with lottery tickets;
and live forever
downwind from the disaster.

Signs of trees but no trees;
images of water but nothing clear to drink.
They burn at the sight of beauty;
are reckless without cause,

rational without understanding.
Among the owls and bats,
they hang from buildings and bridges,
for nothing has been saved for the winter

and summer is but half constructed.
The opossum dances with his mistress,
as the priest with his god;
the rabbit with its mechanic,

as the needle with its habit.
For a suckling child shall lead them
through the streets of Mexico City.
Though the amusements are shuttered,

and the wind burns cold,
the sands of Coney Island
shall be flames of amazement.
For when their forests are bare,

a child will write them back into existence,
one branch at a time,

until the wilderness fills with words
and Gödel's theorem is enacted.

Gödel is consistent:
how shall we incomplete him?
        Gödel, Gödel, teakettle,
            what was the future today?

How can we be one,
now that mastery's gone?
What rights must we wrong?
What songs have we unsung?

The Body's Uncontested Need to Devour: An Explanation

Major Jackson

I am bathing again, burying my face
into the great nations of moss.
I am leaning in, smelling the emerald mountains
and the little inhabitants crossing
over rock-like boulders and tree trunks empired
bit by bit. My nose must come to them
like a probing spaceship causing a mighty eclipse.
They speak in whispers but do not shriek
when gazing into the dim landing bays
of my cavernous thoughts. I am grazing
like a Dionysian. I come not with religion.
I come yearning for first spring and a thirst for spores
pooling like mercenaries in the dark.
The little gods of the forest live here.
I want to ingest their verdant settlements
until they carpet my cavities and convert my raptorial
self into its own ecosystem, off into the green.

The Augury of Birds

W. Luther Jett

Unexpected rain falls and in the high
branches birds flutter to roost —
songbirds, indistinguishable against
grey distance; crows, beaks open
to sound an unheard warning.
There darts a jay, bolt of blue amid
the needles of the near pine.
Rain does not stop this parliament;
their little lives go on, autumnal
migrations continue, star-bidden.

What Tremendum, what untold
catastrophe dares silence the songs
of birds, stills them in their flight?
We who scatter bones in dust
know augury is not enough.
The waters rise and we
imagine we will not drown.

Sarangee*

Krishna Mohan Jha

Maybe the man who discovered this sound
Was deaf from birth
And spent years wandering from jungle to jungle
Searching for his own voice.
Or, to pay for transgressing a royal decree
His tongue was sliced off
And the writhing of his pain-wracked body
Rose up to his mouth and came out unformed.
Or, as inconsequential as a snail
A tidal wave tossed him onto an island of destitution
And the cry of his frothing heart, trembling
Broke on his every breath
Or, someone who lost his home and loved ones
Discovered this sound with his weeping.
In this unfathomable life
Are so many occasions of rupture and loss
that the mother of this sound's birth could be anything,
From the death of a bird to the razing of a slum.
So
In honour of the humanity of those
Who have endured only grief in their lives
Bind up your loincloths and listen
This is no musical instrument
Irrigated by the ascending scale of happiness
It is a glacier of misery built up over centuries
Now slowly melting in its own passion.

---

* Translated from the Hindi by Robert A. Hueckstedt

Making a Chair

Dileep Jhaveri

Making a chair is the most natural thing
and very easy

You can wait for autumn
for every leaf to fall
or you can pluck out the leaves one by one
like a crow picking on mouse flesh
Pull down the tree like an elephant uprooting
and remove the twigs like a wolf tearing at the tendons
Split it apart like a crocodile cracking the bones
Bore in holes like a woodpecker
Fixing crosses and hammering nails is an ancient art
Make the surface smooth with putty provided by the pulp
Obtain paints from the very ancestors of the trees
buried for billions of years to re-emerge through oil wells
Resins from the freshly peeled bark will provide the sheen

Now sit back on the chair set in the veranda
and contemplate over the sprouting green of a grass blade
from a crack in the asphalted pavement
Patiently awaiting a forest

Cell

Deryn Rees-Jones

Imagine a landscape folded into a room:
moonlight like mist on the hills,

blackthorn and alder, the whole world pressed inwards,
a flower between the pages of book.

Imagine then that room became
a microscopic cell, the walls and pages yours and mine: *a stone, a*
   rock, a tree.

Look, you are saying, it dreams us.
Like that night we slept in different rooms, a nucleus of

shadow. Let me run my hands
across the shadows now, the semi-permeable space between:

black hills, bright fields, and stars,
the silence of the pipistrelles.

*

Moonlight like mist on hills,
the whole world pressed between the pages of book.

Imagine this landscape slipped into a room, imagine then a
   tiny cell,
these walls and pages, yours

and mine: a place we might inhabit.
See how the memory dreams us:

the nights we lay awake in separate rooms played over now
and over. Let me run my hands against the nucleus of shadows.

Tonight perhaps the pipistrelles. The fields. Those stars.

Brushing Yonder*

Jill Jones

If you go north, it will get worse.
Valleys won't aid you.
The sun always goes down.
If you go west, you'll stumble.
All that reticence is fooling your shoes.
The moon hides in trenches.
If you go south, you'll drown, eventually.
You'll swell, you'll swivel, then flail
and capsize. It's always stormy.
If you go east, you'll survive.
But scarcely. There's no food.
The greens are dying, substances
rise and cover up the sky.

What if you stay here?
The hedge is full, the air blooms.
We're shot with care and perfume
of bare living, as roses rustle
parrots mass in yonder.
I could take your arm, nothing
banishes sorrow but that's no matter.
How root lives with skin
is the argument. There's always more
where apricots fall and lemons are flush
when you can almost believe, though
that's not enough.

---

* First published in *Brink*, Five Islands Press, 2017

It's what is more certain like a sun
like a phase, like a trice, a sudden brush
of direction. To dream of escape is
to form up the real and open your eyes
as if it was—again—morning.

Different Poems*

S. Joseph

The ploughman's poem:
He covers the field with
cow-dung and leaves
and levelling it he returns.
The sky gets busy drawing
in the muddy puddle
with its slanting coconut trees.

Turn your head a bit,
and you will see the washer woman
through the plantain trees.
The toddy tapper on the palm
takes up the rhythm of her washing.
Clothes hear even in their sleep in the sun.

One of the poems of the forest-dweller
is to smell out an elephant
from a handful of earth.

The mason looks at the stones
and the stones look at him.

Does the boatman write poetry?
For, he draws a wrinkled circle
with the water that he
scoops out of the boat.

---

* Translated from the Malayalam by K. Satchidanandan

Will a tin-pot be poetry
for one out of sex-work?
Yes. Since she has found another life.
The beggars' poetry is
to have to point to themselves
without fingers.

One may think
the grave-digger has no poetry.
He is singing, *all our hopes get buried*
In the churchyard's six feet of earth.

The field is ripe for harvest.
Reaping is poetry,

to be sitting, tired from reaping,
in the shade of the coconut tree,
to be drinking water.

Natural History

Katia Kapovich

We have destroyed too many lands,
murdered too many seas.
Where else do you think we can go on hence?
Why, to the natural history museum!
So here we are, a handful of spectators,
simpleton eyes brimming with tears.
And as our tears turn into seas,
we morph into blue, blue whales,
and the whole world is renewed,
and the air smells fresh, smells good
and sparkles crystal clean.
For what is nature but grace of God
wherein you are a pilgrim?

Talking to Animals

Vincent Katz

I've started talking to animals
I told a deer today have a good day be safe
and I said to a squirrel the same to you
stay off the road

I'm entering the spirit realm
I talk to animals and I think they understand

In a Book

Christopher (Kit) Kelen

are certain heavens
more than gods count

as in the pages of the tree
which tells its years in standing

Chlorophyll of Poetry*

Sachin Ketkar

Icy green blood
From the carnage of multitudinous
Trees, innocuous and mute
On my bare naked hands

Whenever with my sharp pen nib
I lacerate
The white backs
Of a blank sheet of paper
I calligraph cold-blooded lines
Of tongueless poems
On the cemeteries of voided spaces
Vacated by annihilating
Thousands of forests

Unsuspectingly
My hands become part of the conspiracy
Denuding this planet
I too become a collaborator
In this felony

But my lush green hands
Cloaked in the bleeding screams
Of the handicapped trees
Are long-familiar

----
* Translated from the Marathi by the poet himself

152

With the yellow grief
Of a leaf nipped off

The crimson excruciating pain
Of a crushed petal

The wet sting of a branch being broken
The earthy agony
Of being uprooted

These are the very things
Flowing out on the white corpses
In the form of chlorophyll
Of poetry

Ode to the Scarce Yellow Sally Stonefly

Sarah Key

Your silly name, what a twister!
It tickles my tongue,
your criss-cross of veins
braids your translucence

in the tiniest burst—
Scarce Yellow Sally Stonefly—
let's quip your pale wings!
You are rarer than the Rio Grande

siren, that nocturnal salamander
run off by bad run-off.
How scarce is part of your name!
Oh, yes, Scarce Yellow Sally Stonefly,

you have a super-fan,
your stalker and savior
Mr. John Davy-Bowker,
a super-sleuth hero

tracks your species by environmental DNA.
Anywhere you creatures might crawl,
he follows your genetic scrawl
with no cameras or nets.

Hold back your sally for
your nymphs need more oxygen,

alas, the waters are muddied
in the Kingdom of Gwynedd.

Who sullied the Welsh River Dee,
where you were last seen? Where
did you go for twenty-two years?
Thank Davy-Bowker,

following the footprints
of your eDNA, turbid waters be damned!
Though few, he found you,
Scarce Yellow Sally Stonefly!

Tell me, flighty friends, will there be
a Mr. Davy-Bowker for me?
Will some AI god come along, algorithm my scent,
go where my species has gone?

Madame Berthe's Mouse Lemur

Mimi Khalvati

We should have been lemurs, lowering our metabolism
to suit, going into torpor in the cool dry winter months

to save on water and energy. We too should have sailed
on a raft of matted leaves out of poor Africa, out to Madagascar

into a forest of mangrove and thorn scrub, feeding off gum,
sweet larvae sugars, bedding down in tree holes *en famille*.

The very smallest of us, the veriest Tom Thumb, the most
minute pygmy, *tsitsidy*, *mausmaki*, itsy bitsy portmanteau,

little living furry torch, eyes two headlamp luminaries, front
a bib of chamois, tip to tail—and mostly tail—barely as long

as the line I write in, despite illegal logging, slash and burn,
would survive longer than many folk, especially in captivity.

Only the barn owl, goshawk, to watch for in the dark—raptors
with their own big beauty. But Madame Berthe's Mouse Lemur

is caught in the act—a chameleon clasped in her hands,
a geisha lowering her fan: the smallest primate on our planet.

Cyclone Son-in-Law

Ashwini Kumar

The sky was filled with cinnamon clouds
Earth shattered by ferocious sesame winds.
He came without any debris or disaster
Rushing through cataract corn fields.

Walking behind me
He entered like a late-night traveller.
Waiting in her favourite georgette saree
My mother opened the door
Peppered him with flavoured rice and marigold seeds.

Giggling at his weather-greyed curly hair locks
My eleven sisters burst into gales of prairie songs.
He gave everyone salty perfume, and giant prawns
He had brought from the ghost islands of Pacific sea.

Gossiping about frog babies in rain forests,
He suddenly grew nostalgic
Repented flattening tree after tree in anger.
He was tired—his concave eyes were swollen.
He sunk deep in the reclining sofa
Unburdening himself in an untimely nap.

Our losses were many, some irreplaceable, still
My sisters and I wished he could stay longer.
But he was weakened by guilt in his heart
Leaving his old horoscope in my hands, he
Slowly whirled off the window
Promising he won't harm anyone in future . . .

Tree*

Nilim Kumar

The tree entered the municipal office'
It started crying over the mayor's table
with restive jerks.
The mayor's room was
covered in fallen leaves.
His glass-table gleamed
with the tree's teardrops

Then the tree moved out,
its eyes moving
towards some alley-way.
The whole city was overwhelmed
The story of the mysterious tree
became the talk of the town
Every breath of the evening
Carried the fragrance of the tree.
Every ear was excited by
the rustle of the tree.
Curiosity robbed men
Of their sleep
The tree appeared
Even in their dreams

#
One day
the tree descended into

---

* Translated from the Assamese by Upal Deb

158

the city's oldest
abandoned well
It washed its limbs and
headed towards
the insomniac rocks
of the hill it had left.

Hugging the tree's feet
the rocks began sobbing.
But the uprooted tree
slept leaning against the winds
They left the tree
To the mercy of the forest,
with clouds for company.
Other trees whispered
about the strange tree.
Birds and bees followed.
Fallen leaves and insects
joined the gossip.
The whole forest was thrilled
by their whisper.

#
The tree began changing
its colour.
One day it left the forest
with its face hidden,
past the rocks' pallid looks.
It again moved towards
the city,
washed its limbs in the dead well

Entering the municipal office
the tree spread its hair across
the mayor's table.
The flowers in its hair
submerged the table
in violet waves
Everywhere it was
violet violet violet violet
violet violet violet violet . . .

Forest Deliverance

Sukrita Paul Kumar

Following the scent
of the forest and
trailing the whistling wind
that blows through
crisp crunchy leaves
I reach paths
with no destinations

and submit to
the continuities of
morning rays

I move on
guided by mirages
real and vibrant,
not untruths
nor hallucinations;

With the crimson sun
and the silver moon
filling my eyes
I do not see
slithering reptiles,
nor the scowling devils
on the hanging branches above
or the bushes below

my soul lifts me
into the abstraction of the skies
above the clouds
till I cross all borders,
life meets death
and I find myself

couched in my
grandmother's lap
with my eyes, ears and mouth
stretching wide open .

as she starts, yet again,
Once upon a time . . .

Between Species

Susanna Lang

'. . . *eavesdropping gray squirrels respond to "bird chatter" (contact calls emitted by multiple individuals when not under threat of predation) as a measure of safety'*—PLOS One, 4 September 2019*

If squirrels and chipmunks eavesdrop on songbirds to learn
when to hide from a circling hawk and when it is safe

to forage, who might listen to our conversations?
What can sparrows steal along with the crumbs

they scrounge from beneath our café tables? Which human
syllables have starlings woven into their songs?

Could raccoons sift through our murmured words at night,
even our dreams, as well as our garbage? What clues

has the cricket, perched in the rafters of our garage,
gleaned from our comings and goings? A few sanderlings

run the length of this empty beach before
they pause to notice me—and then take flight

toward the south, twittering to those nearby, seen
and unseen, that someone is asking too many questions.

---

* https://journals.plos.org/plosone/article?id=10.1371/journal.pone.
0221279

A Bad Year for Tomatoes

Hiram Larew

Nothing turned red in time
   or swelled as was expected

The piddling August take—
   its drooping nobs
   or oozy spots—
The ants seemed rushing for them.

What early hope there was
   in eager June
   with lush and vines and rooted wild
And stalks tied up from over-grown
with ready jars for putting—

How foolish first our grinning
   in leafy June
   that ended on such little pips
   and scant as screech and fallens off

A lesson-peek at forward harms—
   a yellow time of wanting.

Osprey

B.J. Lee

We tamed the world, I know.
It needed to be done, because . . .
well, there must have been a reason.
It frightened us, perhaps.

December comes in with mild air,
soft breezes over a captured inlet
of still water.
Somebody rolled the sun in gauze,
its fire muted; a clever bit
of engineering.
Sit quietly, listen:
machines hum behind the scenes
keeping it all in place.

Twilight descends across the inlet.
A lamppost's gentle glow
unfurls over shadowed depths.
An osprey perched on her post
beats powerful wings,
then plunges toward the water's surface.
There are no screams
while the world shatters in unstrung fragments.

On Returning from a Trip to West Virginia the Father Brings His Daughter a Jar of White Lightning *Or* Sicilian-American Tough Love

Tim Liardet

'. . . All I got was this lousy moonshine,' you say,
but something in that clear-standing liquefaction
magnified by the curvature of its jar
talked of intimacy as a mischief, an in-joke;
it was a nod to yes as much as nod to no,
a blessing to moody, monstrance to happy;
assent to you as son, as much to you as daughter.
Less than thirty days old, the moonshine dreaming
the tank of some hillbilly bucket of rust
jacked up on bricks with catchweed for blinds,
was as limpid as ether, forty percent pure;
it was as ominous as the devil's bathtub gin,
its depths of ions sparkled, its gases rose,
explained by spilt light. World, be pleased
with what you throw. Amazonian tribesmen,
warily, wade the river to be offered gifts.
A trio of craters gaping a hundred meters wide
surfaces, in North Siberia. And here is love
in its plainest state, securing its vapours
with a screw-thread, marked at eighty proof.

The Company of Trees

Maria Lisella

Under my window, a hushed whooshing sound reminds me I
    may not be alone. They
don't snore but trees creak and groan, slumber and droop at
    nightfall as we
do. Imperceptibly trees breathe deep in calm darkness when
    creatures from mice to
sparrows fade into nocturnal hideouts ready to rise at the first
    sign of light, and
warmth, some survive plagues, pandemics; inherit the earth.
    Some subsist on the
glue on the back of a postage stamp; they, too, rustle in near
    silence below my
window on this summer solstice night that will fade into day as if
    night never came
while I waken just as the trees' branches angle once again to capture

The Cross of History*

Nikola Madzirov

I dissolved in the crystals of undiscovered minerals,
I live among the cities, invisible
as the air between slices of bread.
I'm contained in the rust
on the edges of the anchors.
In the whirlwind I am a child
beginning to believe in living gods.
I'm the equivalent of the migrant birds
that are always returning, never departing.
I want to exist among the continuous verbs,
in the roots that sleep
among the foundations of the abandoned houses.
In death I want to be
a soldier of undiscovered innocence,
crucified by history
on a glass cross through which
in the distance flowers can be seen.

---

* Translated from the Macedonian language by Peggy and Graham Reid

The Grandmother of The World

Charlotte Mandel

One day, the Grandmother of the World stood up.
The old giant harvested her trees grown higher than redwoods.
She filled a burlap bag the size of a mountain with every fruit
in the world.

With a corn-husk rope, she tied the bag onto the back of the cow
with rainbow eyes, taking care not to hurt the great pink
milk-bag. Leading the cow, she strode across the ocean
to the continent where she'd left her sons and daughters
to work for themselves.

She found the earth made of broken concrete, the trees
twisted into barbed wire. People had ripped holes
in each other's bodies. And nobody fed the children.
The children had lost their screams and lay in heaps,
silently turning into shredded paper.

In anger, the Grandmother of the World tore the concrete
hide off the earth, shook her mangled sons and daughters
until they collapsed into fat roots that fell into the new loam.
Green seedlings shot up at once.

And she began to feed the children with milk, and fruit, and cereal.

A Time for Bees

Herbert Woodward Martin

It was a time for bees,
a gathering of pollen,
a dance of honey.
The backyard was
a jungle of wild
things attacking
and spreading havoc
from blossom to blossom.
Witness the quiet activity,
petal to flower, stem to stalk,
the sad leavings of love,
a rock thrown against the night,
a violent interruption of lovemaking,
that excellent moment when
terror knocks upon the door and whispers:
May I come in?

Eel, Siren[*]

Stephen Massimilla

from the icy seas
who shakes off the Baltic
to rejoin our shores, our estuaries, our rivers,
plunging under an opposing
pulse into another intensity
where life branches, artery to artery,
vein to vein, rooting ever deeper into the heart
of the rock . . . filtering
through slimy capillaries until, one day,
forked fires striking though the chestnut trees
will ignite a quiver in clots of dead
water trickled from the towering cliffs
of the Apennines to Romagna:
Eel, torchlight, whip,
Cupid's arrow in the earth
which only our mud-cracked Pyrenean
gutters can ditch-deliver
to the paradise of fecundity;
green fighting industry, probing
for life where the Rubicon is pulled
into a pillaged underworld;
the spark that says

---

* This poem appeared in *The Plague Doctor in His Hull-Shaped Hat*. Stephen
F. Austin University Press, 2013.
Loosely after Montale
[Today, Savignano sul Rubicone is an industrial town; the Rubicon has
become one of the most polluted and diminished rivers in Romagna,
practically eliminated by the exploitation of groundwater.]

to make an end is to begin
where everything is charred,
this twig in its grave,
this rainbow, brief twin
to iridescence under your lashes
flashing in the center
of the empire of your eye,
streaming light to the sons of men;
immersed in your bank of mud—in this, can't you
recognize your *sister*?

Plainsong of the Undiscovered

Glyn Maxwell

You who go in search
with a lantern and a staff
in the dark that you consider
to be dark that wishes only
    to be scattered by your lantern
may we ask you to remember you are

visible for miles
have been visible to us
from the dark that you consider
to be dark we are observing
    the decisions of your lantern
but what's scribbled by a sparkler wasn't

scribbled there for long
like it wasn't true for long
in the dark that you consider
to be dark we're all around you
    so why don't you shade your lantern
let your aching eyes accustom to the

peace before the thought
in this peace we congregate
from the dark that you consider
to be dark we wish to tell you
    you have no need of a lantern
if you come for us the way we say to

come for us like you
come for us like all of you
for we suffer and we wonder
where we meet we suffer wonder
    we have always been the same
and by that we mean the same as always

changing with the light
and we will not come to light
if you come with black-or-whiteness
do not come with black-or-whiteness
    come with everything between
come with everything there might have been and

bring some who won't come
also some who are long gone
bring the jesting and the yawning
and the reckless and uncaring
    you have been what they have been
come with everyone you never think of

then we'll come to light
or what you consider light
come with every kind of colour
colours you don't think are colours
    colours none of you has seen
we shall be where we have always been and

come for us with love
we say come for us with love
if you do not understand love

it is dark where you are looking
    we say good luck with your lantern
in a cell that's got no doors or windows

we are leaving now
we may never catch your eye
but we bide and we are hopeful
not for anything just hopeful
    we'll be hopeful if you find us
we'll be hopeful if you never find us

you who go in search
with a lantern and a staff
through the dark that you consider
to be dark we have departed
    and we bless your tiny lantern
from a distance none alive can fathom

Why Madwoman Shouldn't Read the News

Shara McCallum

I know you'll say I'm overreacting,
but my mother's prophesying has come to pass:
Armageddon is upon us. Just look at the evidence:
the carriers of our species at every second
being raped and killed and the rare ones
who survive offing their lovers and children
(or worse, if it can be believed, wearing bangs),
molesters and gun-toters skulking
in every lunchbox, the environment
churning into an apocalypse. Oh, kids,
please save us the heartache and leave
in advance: calmly but quickly
abandon your seesaws and swings. Friends,
do you remember when we were young?
Life plump with promise and dreams?
Me neither. Anyway, who'd be naive enough
now to believe in anything so impossible-
to-attain as happiness or justice? Sure
we had a run of it. Even some laughs.
But the day's arrived, as deep down we knew
it would, and spectacles streaming
from across the globe should convince
even the most skeptical of our soon-extinction.
Not that we listen to true madmen
anymore, but the older I get
the more certain I become: my father

would have been heralded a prophet
had he lived, would have joined his brethren
and sistren on every street corner, trumpeting
this end from the beginning.

In Other Words

Bruce Mcrae

The wheel of the Earth.
That which brings itself into being.
A night purpled with the blood of the stars,
planets and diamonds exchanging places.
And a kerfuffle in the mighty shuffling.

Where two into one will not divide
and lovers share botched equations.
The man, with thumbprints where eyes ought to be,
his dreams coming into existence.
The woman, climbing out of a halo of light,
pure light tainted by the smoke of the moon.
A red night shaking its rag at love's fool.
A blue night, without tangents or sines.
Green nights becoming invisible,
like radio frequencies or streams underground.

And this room, this ball of time.
A dot in the immediacy.
The last place you'd look
for sleep's furred corners or human immensity.
Every breath making a sweeping arc.
Then silence.
Then more silence.

Lakeside Walks

Arvind Krishna Mehrotra

This lakeside,
this Inner Mongolia,
where the language spoken
is the one you speak
to yourself when you see,
after a rain shower,
a droplet on a leaf tip
or a snail on its way to somewhere.

2

Every few days
walking under trees
I raise an arm to touch a leaf.
You're slightly
out of reach.

3

By the time we came
it was too late, but this
we knew before we came:
we weren't untouched
by wind and rain, weren't quite
the squirrels in the grass
chasing the other's tail.
The old rain makes the new ground muddy
and we cannot see with this wind in our eyes.

4

A man who looks like a stuffed toy
is sitting at a picnic table. He does not move.
There's an unlit cigarette in his hand.
Across from him is a four-lane highway and a walking path
on which hollow bricks have been dumped to make a wall.
The government does as it likes. It has nothing to hide.
It's been a while since I saw a mongoose.
Recently, she wrote to say that she saw one and mistook it for a cat.
It was big. We write to each other every day.
There's a storm brewing.

The man who looked like a stuffed toy
may not survive
but if I see him again I'll read his thoughts.
Deaths and memories come in no order.
My thoughts he can read here.

5

'There's always room at the top,' said my grandfather
when I ran into him in Washington Square Park. He was eating
        an ice
cream.
It was a hot day.
'Scum rises to the top fastest,' said the landlady to a cousin doing
his articles in London in the Sixties.
The cyclist made as if to kick the street dog giving chase,
        stopping it
in its tracks.

A young man, no shoes, walks about aimlessly, which is the same
    as
purposefully.
A fallen branch blocks the way. I'm forced to step over it.
Love's a form of verse as much as a sonnet, and so long as there
    are
bushes,
ragpickers will never be short of rags to pick.

6

It was raining when I left.
By the time I reached the sun was out.
Where the sun fell the cobbles were dry.
I walked on the dry patches. A man in a reflective jacket
swept the leaves. Yesterday, I'd passed a piebald cow.
It was dead. It wasn't there today.
I passed four dogs. When I saw them again, one of them
lifted its leg at the front wheel of my car.
There was no need to tell you any of this.
Of that which there's no need to tell
is sometimes the most telling.*

7

Short black hair, brown with dust;
leather slip-ons; green flares;
a white shirt that's turned grey, bright ribbons pinned on it;

---

* Editor's note: With reference to the last two lines of poem 6 above,
  Mehrotra says: 'The sentence construction that I had at the back of my
  mind was Wittgenstein's "Whereof one cannot speak, thereof one must be
  silent."'

tied round her head a piece of cloth,
its ends reaching her waist.
She stood before a tree, tapping a plastic bottle,
listening to the music she made.

8

Behind a tree guard of cast-iron lace,
a five-petalled flower of deep pink
with a black centre;
in a brass inkpot on a chest of drawers,
a pinwheel bought
at a fair.
Between the long toes of buttress roots
I saw it growing, the pinwheel flower
that kept spinning
even when there was no wind.

9

I walked for thirty
minutes today;
no, twenty-eight.
Not that it makes
a difference.
Two minutes.
The plant I thought
was roadside greenery
had two flowers: small,
bluish, with a yellow
throat. I have
sent you the pic on

WhatsApp. See if
you can identify it.

10

A poem like a tree
can be dated precisely.
For instance today
I saw a blue
face mask hanging
on a branch.

11

Two mynas, eyes right,
goose-stepping on flagstones.
They'll be around when the goose-steppers
are gone like a drying patch
of rain water
on a park bench.

Glass House—Anthropocene

Monica Mody

I want to rise above my limitations

I want to let bird shapes of words flock together into language
that will change skies

I want courage to let the cross burn

Swoop of crow on branch outside fills me with referred pain

Why am I inside this glass enclosure

To land gently on a branch

to coruscate

I need supple wisdom of a nature being

but nature is burning

I find body itself   tremors running deep   every time

patina of noise on ears

I came in search of home

There is no shape after which I will not dive if on the other side I
may find nature intact

I am like the blind woman who rubs darkness over her face wears
     a face of wail

It is a long way home

I am walking on my hands

          if not in body   in word

               grief entangled in hair

          trickle inhibited by sewage and noise

Sounding sonar hymns inside glass enclosure

          rocking back and forth

Others inside look at me with feral eyes

Only eyes betray their remembering

Who are we when collapsed with earth grief

In panic, I step away   from poem to regular

               consternation   effability of situation

     written in body

Deep nature in retreat   I long   to bury my face in

I leaf through selves   old

plans I had made   lists

topics of sanity

Apathy stares back with white eyes

Death procession approaching   I'd joined death's procession

Do I dare exit this glass house

What will I find there

This is comfortable   see   machine cooling air

I weep   cannot deny

body

needs embrace of Earth

It is soundless

You cannot even tell I am crying

But animal in me is pacing

up and down

up and down

This pacing   it is not someone else's responsibility

It is mine

Bring Us Near Nearer*

Sharmistha Mohanty

not further far
take us close closer
unbuild us
to soil gravel mud
fold back the excess
of cloth so we
may weave again
unmake us
a nocturnal sorrow
opens
over the great river plains
the falcon with a
single wing
flies alongside
move us from unfire
to fire
return stone
to the mountains
unfirm us
the alcoholic stoops low
on his plastic stool
in the middle
of the precarious alleyway
unsure our voices
so we can listen
sometimes

---

* From *The Gods Came Afterwards*, Speaking Tiger, 2019

make us many
the not-one
and only then
make us one
the not-two
take us away from
calculations
so there remain only
near and distant
high and low
early and late
para and *apara*
the front and the back
and the four
directions

Fierce Beauty

John Mole

Curious or indifferent,
either way

the natural world
surrounds us

blind though we've often been
to such fierce beauty.

As Blake saw heaven
in one wildflower

so now let us celebrate
the earth's abundance

and its generative
consolation,

root and branch
becoming blossom

loosened on the air
in purer light.

The Lost Mango Tree

Sonnet Mondal

The mango tree which I reared
is lost today somewhere
in the jungle of my wishes.

I used to throw whole mangoes
in our backyard
to see them grow up into trees.

Not a single leaf sprouted
except from a half-eaten one.

After watering it in its infancy
I became engaged
wining and dining with my life.

After years—today
a mangrove in our backyard
shaded my memories
from the hard sun of forgetfulness.

I wish I had left myself
to the charity of wilderness.

What Colour Is Blue?

Daniel Thomas Moran

There are
those strands
of our reality
which defy our
words.

Limply, they
render answers,
Which simply
refuse
to appease.

I thought that
I knew blue,
Until I chanced
to sail on the
Mediterranean.

Now the bluest
of skies only
disappoints.
It makes me blue
to think about it.

Trapped in
the cage
of our senses,

All is but
air and light,

In a sea of
things which
move inside us,
in colors we are
unfit to describe.

Chorus

David Morley

on the birth of Edward Daniel Keenan Morley

The song-thrush slams down gauntlets on its snail-anvil.
The nightjar murmurs in nightmare. The dawn is the chorus.
The bittern blasts the mists wide with a booming foghorn.
The nuthatch nails another hatch shut. The dawn is the chorus.
The merlin bowls a boomerang over bracken then catches it.
The capercaillie uncorks its bottled throat. The dawn is the chorus.
The treecreeper tips the trees upside down to trick out insects.
The sparrow sorts spare parts on a pavement. The dawn is the
    chorus.
The hoopoe hoops rainbows over the heath and hedgerows.
The wren runs rings through its throat. The dawn is the chorus.
The turnstones do precisely what is asked of them by name.
The wryneck and stonechats also. The dawn is the chorus.
The buzzards mew and mount up on the thermal's thermometer.
The smew slide on shy woodland water. The dawn is the chorus.
The heron hangs its head before hurling down its guillotine.
The tern twists on tines of two sprung wings. The dawn is the
    chorus.
The eider shreds its pillows, releases snow flurry after snow flurry.
The avocet unclasps its compass-points. The dawn is the chorus.
The swallow unmakes the Spring and names the Summer.
The swift sleeps only when it's dead. The dawn is the chorus.
The bullfinches feather-fight the birdbath into a bloodbath.
The wagtail wags a wand then vanishes. The dawn is the chorus.
The corncrake zips its comb on its expert fingertip.
The robin blinks at you for breakfast. The dawn is the chorus.

The rook roots into roadkill for the heart and the hardware.
The tawny owl wakes us to our widowhood. The dawn is the
    chorus.
The dawn is completely composed. The pens of its beaks are dry.
Day will never sound the same, nor night know which song
    wakes her.

On Barren Land Once Forest

Tim J. Myers

This forest came down for popsicle sticks and cardboard
because the Victorians blushed to imagine
their Mother Nature naked, or even a real Woman,
and so made her a minor lady-in-waiting
to their staid bewhiskered old Watchmaker—
no deity even, only a plump and jolly matron
doing autumn leaves in paint-by-number,
chaperone to the svelte sexual fairies of April,
given now and then to pique of drought or flood.

Would the forest stand today,
its sunlight muted and thousand-shaped
by trembling green multitudes,
its mosses savage, wildflowers utterly pagan,
if those dutiful wielders of the might
of the Industrial Revolution

had once glimpsed God and Nature
clasped in naked passion, struggling,
He and She asweat through all eternity?

Chitrakuta*

Vivek Narayanan

And to that mountain paradise set on fire
by the red blossoms of the *kimsuka* tree,
honeycombs hanging like buckets,
marking-nut trees, the cry of the moorhen,
the bleat of the peacock, the herds
of elephants and the echoing of birds,
they arrived with open eyes. Sita
gathered firewood and fruit while the brothers
caught and killed some quick deer, rabbit,
wild fowl. Famished, they ate on the riverbank.
The next day readying for the long darkness
ahead, Lakshmana sacrificed a black antelope
with a splotch of red on the skin between its horns.
Arrows removed, bleeding stanched, the animal
was gently strangled then laid down
with its legs pointing North, then stroked
and pleasured, washed in all the openings
by which its life-spirit had fled: mouth, nose,
eyes, ears, navel, penis, anus, hooves.
In the beginning, the gods accepted man
as victim. Later, the ability to be sacrificed
passed from him into antelope and horse.
From horse into cattle, from cattle
into sheep, from sheep into goat, then from
goats into the earth, so all the world

---

* After Valmiki's *Ramayana: Ayodhyakanda, sargas 55-56 in the vulgate/*Gita
Press edition

was touched by our humility, our
complicity. Outside the leaf-thatched hut,
the animal was raised on a spit and roasted
until it had attained a deep, dark brown colour.
Then, chanting the appropriate verses, taking care
not to split the bones, Rama carved the animal
limb by limb, cut by cut, setting aside the grain
of its hair, the pumice of its skin, taking into him only
the fire of its flesh, the sublime fat of its marrow.

Pobitora

Rimi Nath

The winding trail
Follows me with its ghostly tremor
Of wintry dryness
And fallen papery leaves.
The naked trees lift their pleading arms
To the sky
A host of classical dancers
Graceful in bare beauty.

The smell of the forest
Captivates me for a while
I see a stork
With pleated wings resting on a stone
Embracing a secret life.
Others hunch together
Or fly a little height to rest again.

The magical river and *Mayong* the land of magic
Cast a spell of love
Rhinos feeding their young
Eating without care.
I stare at migratory birds for a while
I have migratory birds for friends.
I look back at the winding trail
It follows me with its rustling love.

January

Robin S. Ngangom

A stranded train of hurt and memory offloads us at winter's coming.
Something freezes birdsong and
We see only ashen arms of woodless trees. And
Even if you hum with cold, January will not leave.
Will the bluebird ever return to the heart's forked branches?
I imagine a world bereft of snow, and
Waiting for the sixth extinction
Watch giant fish beached by plastic.
The time is here for you to forgive me
For wounding the sleeping furry animal of your thighs.
On that road stretched taut between us
Only a mist and granite sadness has remained.
If anyone were so much as to mention a word like 'love'
Everything will fall quietly again as snow.

Our Eldorado

Stanley Niamatali

From the soupy grave
of warm palm oil
and sallow mud,
    eyes closed,
Eldorado rises and,
    from head to toe,
is dusted with finest gold.

From the dank cave,
    between night and day,
Eldorado comes forth,
    the walking relic.

Below,
    the open-mouthed
    black lake sobs softly
    onto the silent sand.

The wind blows,
    and a somber rain falls
    on the swooning trees.

The oblique insipid light
    shows solemn shadows.
Hot tears overflow
    their tender eyes,
    warm their faces
    and melt into the sand.

Through agonizing eyes,
    they behold their dear
    sweet son, a wisp
before the cave of nothingness.

From the black rock,
    quick as a meteor,
Eldorado,
    a burnished flash,
sizzles into the abyss—
    the ripples of a kiss.

Undulating lilies
    waft their essence
    to the rafts where men
    dutifully paddle
to the blooming
watery rose.

There,
    in its radiating center
they cast the anathema,
    uncorrupted gold
into the vaulted
    and alluring depths.

The rain stops;
    earnest supplicants
    break chains,
    unfinger rings,
    unlock bracelets,
all gold,

and cast them
into the gulping
watery lips.

The resolute lake,
      showing nothing of its depth,
      lithographs the boundless sky.
A voluptuous swell
      rolls across its face
      to the shore.

A great big
        and beautiful silverfish,
        streaked with gold, rises.
Her iris,
      a wheel of golden spokes
      sprocketed by a black pearl.
Water, flows over its back,
      mirroring the suddenly golden sun.

The devout prostrate
      on the rafts and sand
      as she disappears to her
Elisium depth.

Opening their dutiful eyes,
      they behold Eldorado
      floating on the lake.

Eldorado,
      his nakedness,
      covered with a rough cloth,

lies on slippery
    green banana leaves.
His mother,
    kneeling,
      breathes into his mouth.
Sacred water gushes
    from his lips as he opens
his brown eyes flecked
with gold.

Glowworms
    punctuate leaves;
the petal-strewn anaconda
    asleep in its hide;
bugs
    embrace twigs;
a frog squats
    on a succulent spine;
marmosets genuflect in trees
    where orchid blooms waver;
oriole
    busy with banana;
corn with silken flax
    roast over ruby coals;
plantain chips bubble
    in palm oil;
a calabash
    of palm wine;
pineapple
    mandalas;
a jaguar dozes
    on a lazy limb;

sunlight pierces the water
    with its crooked staff—
All. All
    auriferous.

And above it all,
    on this land
    that is El Dorado,
the harpy eagle,
    its wings spread
    across the sky,
circles this lost world,
    its forlorn cry a fading wrinkle
    in our twilight paradise.

Rising Heat

Philip Nikolayev

I am, like you, human, a thinking primate
subject to all the scares of modern times.
I fail to put my mind off blinking climate
and other fundamental human crimes;
off how we conquer, greedy and courageous;
off how we burn our fuels as we compete,
compete, compete, compete; off how our wages
are calculated now in waves of heat.
Helpless, afraid, I harbor a grave concern.
What good will poems be evaporated?
What good will the earth be incinerated,
abolished by a burn of no return
in the bronze gut of this Phalarian Bull?
That's what I can't seem to get through my skull.

The Tree
(For Shongdor)

Kynpham Sing Nongkynrih

Some time ago, I planted a friend and a brother
in the fallow field that was my workplace.
I nurtured him daily, watering,
feeding him fresh soil and manure,
pruning his leaves and branches,
even talking to him morning and evening,
as advised by pundits,
so he would grow faster and healthier.
At the end of three years,
he blossomed for the first time,
and people say, look, he is the best thing
that has ever happened to this place.

But before he could fructify,
huge ugly ants nested on his trunk
and caterpillars crawled about his branches.
People say, chop him off,
how can we live with insects crawling about us?

With unbelievable torment, I fetched the axe of anguish.
I spoke to the tree that was my friend and my brother.
Is it my fault that I mean to chop you off
with the very hand that planted you?
Is it your fault that insects are nesting
in your heart and crawling about your limbs?

I spoke to him for a long time.
But when I was done, I found my hand
could no longer move.
Till today the hand and the axe
are still suspended in mid-air.

To the Spring

Jean Nordhaus

Footsteps follow footsteps
single file along the path
past penstemon and scrub oak,
columbine and mallow,
names we learned
from those who walked
ahead. And when
we place our mouths
against the mossy pipe stem,
we are drinking for ourselves
and our return, but also
for the ones we know
will not return, who left
odd flints and jawbones
for our porches, ghostly
flowers in our albums,
and for the ones not yet
arrived, that they may drink
for us who ate the cress
and fished the stream before.

Hurricane Irma

Fan Ogilvie

Strong winds die down,
white pie-plate hibiscus bloom
in perfect form, veins of their wheels
show clearly from the back-lit sun.

Further, in the field, cows and calves
cavort as if in a Corot painting.
Friday morning dawn breaks—
peaceful, windless,

as though earth shook off a strong
hangover now dry refreshed mindful,
with hope to enjoy sobriety another day,
but knows just down the southern

trail a mad wind with monster eye
moves like Leviathan to tear,
to reverse our poor attempts to shelter,
to create one thing that stands.

A Morning Legend*

Amir Or

At dawn a man rose and opened his window:
a line of sun—from east to west!—
it reached as far as his heart and lit his sorrow,
and he said: Beautiful is the world.

And he said: Why was I so bitterly depressed?
What dream passed through me? Let me wake!
I'll create a new world this morning;
I shall be! – there's no other *when*.

I'll rise and go to the world of leaves,
let me touch its green heart!
Like a butterfly I'll flutter among flowers
and suck life's sweet nectar.

He set forth, but not far: ten steps,
a life cleansed of any past,
by dawn he walked against the reddening east,
and his eyes opened and saw.

Ten steps, no more. But for him
longer than his life to that point:
At the moment of nectar,
    who can recognize his yesterday,
who can count ten eternities?

Once upon a time, a man rose at dawn
and emerged to a forgotten Eden.

---

* Translated from the by Seth Michelson

You can write me*

Pratishtha Pandya

If you can speak of rivers
Without bringing in the Sea
Of trees
Without mentioning the fruits
Of jungles without birds
Of clouds without rains
Then perhaps
You can converse with me.
If you can hear,
Amidst leaping waves
And turbulent tides
A bohemian tune
The tinkle of a silver fish's tail
Then perhaps you will hear me.
If you can hear
The moist dark of a tree
Trapped in its leaves
Getting darker by the night
The charcoal dark
Of her deserted nests
Filling the air
After the birds are all gone
The dark dripping
Half-dead
From its fruit-laden boughs;
In the middle of a noisy forest

---

* Translated from the Gujarati by the poet

If you can hear something
Soft, muffled, faint
Almost quiet
Plink . . . plink . . . plink . . . plink . . .
Then perhaps you can catch me
In your palm and gather
And tie the dark
in a dry white cloud.
Then perhaps
You can write me in words
You can write a rain poem

Limit

Alvin Pang

Mounting evidence of 'an existential threat
to civilisation'. Cascading causes and effects,
the hawk crying over a desert freed of words,
a white bear thinned to pity on a sliver of ice.
The 'heads of government' talk the talk
not of risk and shock but impunity regardless:
surviving on top even of a heap of cinders. A tip
pointed at the heart of now: sovereignty. The
climatologists check their fundings again hoping
to be wrong. The winemaker says this is good
for the high end but the bottom tier is drying out,
lacking the margin for water. Why teach the young
this green stuff, the Perm Sec grumbles, it's bad
for business. The bushfire says the same, only
more fiercely. The politicians say—well, just listen.
It's sexy now: time to stock up on solar, galoshes.
Going vegan won't help, warns a new report.
The priests say wait. The *Children of Weather*,
the lovers, would let the world drown just to live
together. It's always about coping against hope.
Not much else to do, being so small. Headlines say
nothing about where the news will stop or what
to do after you've crossed the line at last, the last
real year you felt good in your bones.

The Green Floor

Diane Wilbon Parks

Morning finds a curious sun looking at its reflection
from raindrops perched on leaves dripping of light,
And as these blushing rays untwist their breath onto each leaf,
Silver droplets roll until they reach the earth's floor.
Each raindrop, though small carries an important journey,
Each sun-drenched leaf gives back life.
Oh, what majesty, leaves and raindrops hold in their offerings.
Every natural thing that falls to earth leaves a gift.

The wide spine of a blue sky sees its reflection in a small pond
and notices the spinning clouds lost from its mirrored view.
I am drawn to all of these—the sky, the sun, the birds, the
      damselflies, the meadow
And its tall green grass that shoots up out the earth and into my
      pockets,
Every shiny blade sweeps across my waist, and paints my legs green.
I lay on the belly of the earth, its skin covered in green
and pluck things from the earth that will cause it to fade.
So much of what I see does not belong here,
I peel old papers hiding just above the soil, the plastic caps, the
      old bottles
and every un-Godly thing that lingers in this sacred place.

Where will sunlight go if it does not slip into the soft ears of
      humanity?
What will shoot up out of the seed of our being?
We must bend forward with knees pressed into the ground,
to become green like the meadow.

We will need to wait like trees, like plants and flowers
for the sun, the wind, the rain and the seasons to come and feed
    like a father.
We will need to grow a blue sky in us like a mother.
We will need to take our shoes off, plant our feet like children,
and walk a mile in the root of trees.

Journey

Sabine Pascarelli

Come autumn, I wonder if trees would like
to pack their bags and wander off to visit their
cousins, scattered in the southern regions of the world—

take their leave before the shedding of the leaves,
with the first harsh cries of geese, following
the swirl of hummingbirds, south, south.

We'd see them crowding stations, airports, harbors,
to take a trip, just once a year, close the doors behind
and see the world with its content of dreams

unfolding. Unknown landscapes, different air.
How would it be to see the sunburned, southern soil being
penetrated by a vast network of roots of giant oaks, firs,

cypresses, maple trees? Songbirds nesting in their shaded
branches, sweet song filling the desert's void?
The gods would surely soften, moved by such a beauty,

and send warm rain. Can you imagine? Just 2-3 months
a year. How would it feel to look at barren landscapes,
all trees gone – How could they do that to us?

Green

Linda Pastan

Nothing is left
but green.
Forsythia,
dogwood, lilac
each has had its turn
and faded out.
Even the red maple
is green.

There is only texture now:
the green magnolia leaves
smooth as sea glass,
the prickly green of ferns,
and always those rough green
armies of grass.
For chlorophyll itself
is on the march,

has gone viral,
its pigments stain
the very motes of air.
Be careful where you walk,
or you may drown
in green. The tide
of summer is finally
cresting.

I've Come This Way So Many Times Before . . .
And I've Never Seen You

Keith Payne

We are making a detailed inventory
like the herbarium of an unpredictable constellation.
First of all the lilies, flourish to the raining stars,
the dahlias and chrysanthemums,
and don't leave out the poppies, those shy, tiny flowers
must also be counted.
The flower of the fig tree is subliminal.
The wallflower the most bookish of all.
The orchid is clearly a lascivious flower,
It's a little bit like the . . . no, I'll not go on.
Hibiscus fills the evening with wit and whimsy.
Hydrangea: tell me how happy I have been here.
There's the iris, lavender, the so-called tea rose.
And then the magnolia that, as its name surely suggests
must once have been the emblem of some Mongol dominion.
The calla lily, anemones and the hardened note of the
        rhododendron.
And then the wonders from far off,
the unspeakable flower of the chilamate
that you feel but never see,
like the deep love that rises throbbing from your feet.
And then
the white lily, the old blush rose and dandelions.
We have cosmos and sage and impatiens but these are
more conceptual flowers.
The passionflower is the throne of an answer,

the baldachin of deliberation.

There are flowers that hold the name of the first eye that ever
    saw them.
Lilacs, calendula, marigold.
I can't forget the mimosas, the swarm of tiny warnings,
or the one I idolize the most: the bougainvillea's outrageous
    clamour.

But, as I've said,
it's odd, I know . . .
I've come this way
so many times before and . . .
no,
I've never seen you
ever.

Poem 1

Erin Petti

You were only a nearly dead bird
Who came to be my daughter.

Bones met at indelicate angles
And behind your neck, flesh torn by my teeth.

My heart could never stop aching.

Paleolithic wings at once
Turned to arms
Spindling, bent.
Frosted beak to lips and nose.
There, a girl.

You were only a nearly dead bird.

Clouds*

Blas Munoz Pizarro

Clouds pass over the world. Go
Indifferent to their Good, oblivious
To their harm. Light, almost motionless,
Reproduce the detached dreams

Of the man who looks at them. Other times,
Extend with their eyelids closed,
Gray wings of a dream without dreams,
Over the dark silence of life.

Clouds pass under the ceiling
Of a blue, unattainable sky. Are
hostages to the light, daughters of the day.

In them we contemplate fate:
Get there, free without being, to our night
In the invisible Flow that takes us

---

* From *The Wound of the Days*, translated from the Spanish by Jaime B. Rosa

Far from the Skyline*

Sharmila Pokharel

Like an old melody still in memory,
as a secret story inside the heart,
the bamboo trees in my backyard,
the mango trees in my front yard.

The land that grows
thousands of papayas and *lichis*,
the soil that flourishes marigolds and lilies.

O, my childhood land,
if I come back
will you still embrace me
as you did before?

Do you still have
the giant *simal* tree
on the roadside?

Do you still carry
the smell of jasmine flowers
all over the village?

---

* Published in *Somnio; The Way We See It*, a poetry and art book project

Confluence

Rochelle Potkar

Waters when they evaporate, meet . . .
at a global conference, to speak of fish dropouts,
obscura of clouds, near-deaths, hydrological dynamics,
monocultures, and metals:
nickel, lead, chromium, at their beds.

The bend is notional: water for coffee, cane,
banana, paddy,
mills, distilleries,
fertilizer plants.

The Aral sea was water for cotton
in Uzbekistan:
one shirt drinking 2000 liters,
now more saline than the Dead Sea—
palm-sized, a fossil-tiger's footprint,

plains of salt, toxic dust storms,
fishing towns, now ship-graveyards.
people, sick; dumps of pathogenic weapons
making the summers hotter, winters colder,
the Aral sea is the Aralkum desert.

And if seas made maps,
rivers, homes
men, borders.

The Cauvery too is uprising
—one of the longest-running rivers
over her water share to ripple greens
for Karnataka and Tamil Nadu,
when her sand beds expand for mining
flowing from Brahmagiri
on her way to the Bay of Bengal,
she worries if those warring over her understand

that a river is a person,

like Whanganui of New Zealand
—ancestor of 140 years
that got legal status
through the longest-running litigation
by the Māori people

because mountains too
are equal to men.

Playing Hide and Seek*

M.P. Pratheesh

While playing hide and seek,
she presses her face on to the tree
and covers her eyes.

The snake living in the trees hollow
Brushes its poison-teeth

and slithers away
without losing her way.

The tree does not see anyone:
not even the dead child,
not even the curled-up snake.

---

* Translated from the Malayalam by K. Satchidananan

Blood Web*

Q.R. Quasar

'*I put your blood back into your own veins*'
—'Muddy Waters', Mckinley Morganfield

we are all webbed together
    by the salt water of the sea
and we carry the ocean around
      in us
          in the tides of our blood pound

we are all blood-webbed to the sea
    and through the sea to each other
our skein is one ocean
    both on land and in the sea

when we breathe, the ocean breathes
    we are the sea that walks
    (we have no roots like trees)
    we are the sea that swims
we are the blood web
        cast beyond the air
our reach is blood-lined to the voids between . . .

but we can only live in the ocean
so we carry the ocean around

---

* (from They Call Me Muddy Waters

226

in us
in the tides of our blood pound
we are all blood-webbed to the sea
our skein is one ocean

we are all blood-webbed together
    by the salt water of the sea
we are all one ocean, one air, one void
we are all blood-webbed together in the tree
                    of mind
we are all blood-webbed together
we are all one blood-web
we are all one blood-web

* * * * * *

—August 2007 C.E., 2.73° K:
13.8 billion years after the Big Bang (ABB);
Lake Michigan/Atlantic Coast,
the Americas, Earth, Sol System,
        Local Arm, Milky Way, Virgo
        Supercluster of Galaxies
        among 1000-plus galaxy clusters
        caught in the undertow,
        in the Dark Flow,
        streaming towards the unknown . . .
        unseen . . . Even Greater Attractor—
        all in the Web-Weave of Galaxies
        in the voidnest
        here

Solstice Poem

Barbara Quick

How will I spend my last two hours of sunlight,
on this shortest day of the year? Will I gather lemons
before I cover the trees again
against the frost tonight?

Or clear away the raspberry canes
I've been pruning for days now,
separating the quick from the dead?

Or should I simply sit instead, alone
on the pretty painted bench I bought
with thoughts of the friends I would entertain,
six feet apart, in the garden,
in the days before everything
got so much worse—

And slowly eat a small dark chocolate bar
infused with orange rinds while I think about
the friends who've died, and all the dead
who can't be reached.

Homo Sapiens

Ann Quinn

Indian summer, we used to call it, but now whenever the
    temperature
hits ninety in October we see the future we're creating.
Meanwhile the spiders are casting their thick autumn webs,

one such on the line where I'm hanging sheets.
Each silken junction holds a plump amuse-bouche and I'm
    carefully working
around someone's feast, but then my sheet snags the spider

and now the nickel-sized red creature is clambering down the cloth
and I scream and try to shake her off but she drops another thread
anchoring herself to my bedding and now I've mangled her
    endeavor.

I shake the sheet again and drape it, hoping the spider has
    dropped away, or will
but hours later she is still there on the white expanse, folded like
    a DeLorean,
legs neatly hidden. Rather than examine her in her retreat, I find
    a stick

and bat her to the ground, successful this time, oh mighty me.
From the blinded Cyclops, Odysseus stole the sheep.
I fold my laundry and look again at the mangled web,
wishing I'd captured its beauty on my phone when it was whole.

Moony Tunes

Anupama Raju

I

I'm reading a book.
I'm a letter on a page.
I'm part fact, part fiction.
I'm on a train. Train is on its way.
I'm looking out the window,
for purpose, sheep and cows,
I'm on a train to London.
Cows are out grazing.
I'm on a train to the moo moo moon.
It's fine to amble along in poetry,
I hallucinate, I ramble, I sing a moony tune.

II

There's the full moon
eye ball behind
a cataract of clouds
blind harbinger of
what's to come tonight.
Demons, come forth,
werewolves, do not hide,
tear up the flesh
dig into wounds
suck up bones
and every life in sight.

Darling beasts,
don't stay home tonight,

hear the devil prowl
as it begins its hunt tonight.

III

(On nights like this when I look at the full moon and begin a
        poem all I'm trying to do
is really write about the full moon in new ways but there are no
        new ways to write
about the full moon because the moon has been full for centuries
        and there have
been better meditations about it than rants about devils and
        werewolves. All I'm
trying to do is write an unusual poem to surprise you with similes
        and turns of
phrases but end up sounding so profane that the poem is now
        nothing but a cheap
horror flick with bad make-up and terrible actors who put
        ketchup and green goo on
their faces. Poem dead. Moon dead.)

IV

P.S.
The moon has disappeared.
The poem has chased it away.
Shoo.

* * *

Aliso Viejo
Speak to me in the language you speak
the one I don't recognize
the language of wisdom,
the wisdom of hills
in a world of singed hearts
surround me with your winter
the one I cannot feel
the winter of dreams
let me grow roots where you stand
lend me your soil, pull me into your shade
strip, wash and cover me, take my breath
carve me into the Aliso you've been waiting for.

Note: (Aliso Viejo means 'the old Alder tree' in Spanish; it is also
a town in Orange
County, California.)

Mother

P. Raman

To fill
My pitcher
The river needs
Just
A smile

O Wind, O Sea!*

P. P. Ramachandran

Like the bronze water-jug left behind
on the front verandah
instead of being kept safe inside
got stolen,
a hillock by the paddy-fields
vanished at dawn.
Whereall didn't rain and sunshine
look for it!

My house sits
on the hip of a hill
that is still left intact.

Now-a-days
hills are all daily-wagers
working on the highway,
lulling to sleep
the bawling little houses.

Pantalam-hill, Pootra-hill
Puliara-hill, Para-hill,
Chola-hill, Chanta-hill,
Palmyra-hill . . . when the names are
called out from the roster
everyone has to fall in line,
march up to the lorry and board it,

---

* *Translated from the Malayalam by A.J. Thomas*

get down where ordered
and remain standing,
carrying on their flattened heads
the eight-lane Expressway.
Time will go fleeting over their heads
'shooom . . .'
Shouldn't budge!

O Wind, O Sea
O coconut fronds!
We are going to be this side of the Expressway
and you, on that side
Not likely
to see each other again.

Like Narayani in Basheer's story*
who threw a dry twig up into the sky
You too must show some sign:
I'll wait for it.

---

* In the famous story *Walls* by Vaikom Muhammad Basheer, the heroine
Narayani, a prisoner in the women's part of the Central Jail, romantically
inclined towards the hero in the men's prison, throws a dry twig up into
the sky to be seen above the dividing wall, to announce her presence.

From the New World I*

Yaxkin Melchy Ramos

Butterfly in the Rain
The day arrives
when it doesn't matter who I am
nor who I was
nor who I will be
when they all fade like illusions
in watery reflections
like the shapes of clouds
like the sound of a drop of water
and another
Everything is heard
Everything sings its song
Everything sees with its eyes
and savors the water
and is fed by the earth
Everything knows its own scent
and lives and falls away
and dies and is incorporated
It doesn't matter who it was
or what it will be
It matters in the moment
its heart beats
It speaks in the moment
its heart beats
It declares its dream in the moment
its heart beats

---

* Also appears bilingually in Poatechnics (Cardboard House Press, 2021)

It has never lost its origin
it doesn't matter if it's sown
or ignored
The origin returns to itself
like spring
and walks ahead
Why cling to stopping it in its tracks
if the heart breaks free
advances with the spring
lands lightly
on the flower.

Two Poems on the Greening of America

Susanna Rich

Kudzu

Caress, it says, and *caress.*
Rubbish, they call this vine rampaging
ram's head and mitten leaves over power lines,
telephone wires; fence, sign, bush, other vines;
blending all into an ectoplasm of green—

green veils, green hair, green hoods
draping skeletons of choked pine, magnolia, scrub.
Garland, they wanted, *festoon*—
quick cover from Japan to clutch
the earth from encroaching on U.S.

interstates and tracks—our transports of speed.
Then *rampage,* they said, *greed*—
rank treachery to reach for itself,
be sculpted by its own joy and momentary
dips to rain—to flicker its under leaves

at them, finger its way back toward home.
What is this vine but a woman bereft,
who clasps and gathers, dances and weeps?
Who blankets hard edges, thickens
what's fluid—like all that's shunned

enlarging herself for others' displeasure?
Didn't they know it must shrivel
what it shades, smother what it covers—

like shame, bare what is core, hard
true—like long grief, give her own

fullness to redress loss?
Touch, say the winged petals; *be*,
the laden pods. Sister vine, transforming
exile into twining tendrils, hunkering
gorgons, pietàs whispering.

Our Dying Lake

> *For Christina*

—you crawling the quarter mile
to the far shore, ten minutes there—
to my side-stroking sputter
in your wake—not quite to midway.

Twice a week, sometimes three,
through that summer, my car or yours
slaloming holes and boulder crowns,
five miles of backroad dust, basking rattlers.

I was content to watch you unzipping
the water, foam at your feet,
the silver flicks of your elbows—
your breath echoing from the cliffs.

By August, I, too, crawled across, sunnies
nipped, one saddled me for a thrash.
Dragonflies motored, swallows looped.

Our blue heron, Jazz, posed among lilypads.

We skimmed the depths, breast-stroked
the narrow corridors of lifting fog,
dodged the rare jig-sawing snake.
October, online neoprene swim-skins,

we tempted lowering temperatures—
82, 60, 52—43 on November 28th.
We swam in a December flurry; then
blasted the car's hot vent into our armpits.

Christina, toxic emerald algae now raft
our silver waters because of global warming.
Mustn't touch the lake. Mustn't breathe its mists.
The cliffs echoes wind. No eagles wing above us.

When the Slope

Santiago Rodriguez

When the slope is burnt harder
The lea grass springs greener. Cowboys
know it, those who throw their writings, their future,
To the fire. There is no sacrifice
Without retrieval nor smoke without embers,
because the flower does not tell lies. Its beauty remained,
if it was it will comeback, reborn, someone will have
To rescue it getting rid of himself. The seed gives itself
And perpetuates itself, sprouts,
to cover the rags of time, as Donne said.
In any mountain spring lies
Mystery, creation. The words
You heard are repeated lies,
Commodities, artifice. You see, what is natural
Flows, occurs; the combination,
Devoid of interpreters and rhetoric, arises
And it is fine as such. And may it pass. So that flowing away
Means no return, such a pity the river
That has been a spring, such a pity.
I know that the spring is there, in the spot
Where the watercress clusters, because its vigor
From purity comes. That it does not hide at night
Or in the deep, that if it were clean one would see
The water flow out in the surface,
Swirling the slime. I know I could remove
The watercress easily and when the mud clears

My sight would revel in gushes, as my desire of possession
Would come true. And of dominion. I also know
That that which destroys, changes. That which you may
Reject is you.

Stream Channelization

Bobby C. Rogers

The water had it right, but our ideas ran contrary. In draining the
    Beech River bottom, crooked feeder streams got turned into
    ditches
as straight as the Army Corps of Engineers could dig them. To
    a farmer's eye, the regularized land looked like money. What
    good was anything
if you couldn't grow it in rows? Simplify, simplify. You can
    smell the resentment in the de-featured fields, the ground
    embarrassed
to be stripped of its hardwoods and still water, ridded of winter
    waterfowl, scarred by a ditch as inerasable as the crease in an
    old letter

set to fall apart from one more reading. It's wrong to be in love
    with such simplicity. Water wants to bend and meander. We
    were supposed to be
hunting, but my mind always wandered, thinking about how we
    believe we don't need to change but the land does, about how
    we've failed to honor
the water's wishes, how a straight line is the least lovely distance
    between two points. We tramped past a family grave plot so
    long undisturbed
it'd become a waist-high hillock risen from the eroded field,
    crowned with broom sage that moved when the wind moved
    and illegible tombstones that didn't.

We will Be a Source and the Source will Return*

Jamie B. Rosa

We will be a source again
and the source will be again,
after his exile

Our river
Sea sea that by opening the way
you are our guide
from the first threshold
to the last door
and you under the arches
that support us
bring us promises
for there is a sweet
and even flame in you
In which mirror will
forever be reflected
the bright horizon that
awaits us?

There are amphorae of
triple doubt in your transparency
As wastes there are
in the best angle of being,
with rumors and litanies
with measure and compass

---

* Translated from the Spanish by Nishi Chawla

long as snakes with sweet urine
that govern the meanders of the verb

Goddess of the waves
and the needles that weave the sea
May the alchemical light
of your being shine on all things
and evil wills!
For in You
the sea is clear and does not betray
for his false glass eye
Slow wave and letter
that you adorn when you
sign up on the shores!
Will your breath
save the perfect form that we are?
Fire goddess of woman
and sweet aroma
that expresses itself in the wave
and expands on the shore
Guide our long way!
What strange being was
more contrary to the silent light
under the stubborn pain of the world?
That with your transparency
you elevate us beyond where
the wing is imposed
and let us contemplate
those golden spaces from above
where the fruit sleeps
and sprouts with

the brilliance that unfolds
in the flowers

In the truncated hills
dwells the eye of an archangel
as oblique ceremony of
a something that does not listen
although round is
the fence and the fragile feather
What about us Goddess!
The stubborn shadow of
evil turns away
with the austere sail
through the night valley
although the cry is contrary to us
and its flaming shards of shrapnel

And like beings born of the mud
let us be silent on
the eternal mattress of liquid doubt
that doubt that is nothing
when the truth is spelled out
for everyone

The Isle of Light*
(for Varavara Rao)

Gabriel Rosenstock

There is an Isle of Light
I will take you there
It has never known iron bars
Come with me to the Isle of Light

There is no government there
The seas rule and the ocean winds
Seasons change at the word of poets
Come with me to the Isle of Light.

---

* Translated from the Irish by the poet

Elegy For the Dusky Seaside Sparrow

Michael Rothenberg

Take note:

Rock Hudson died of AIDS.

Rita Hayworth's picture was pasted
                on the first Atom Bomb.

Yul Brynner died the day my father died,
                Orson Welles a week after.

So what about the Dusky Seaside Sparrow?
Extinct in the middle of June,
                nineteen hundred and eighty-seven.

It's a Disney World
        of space shuttles and evolution.

But this heart of mine
wants to stop.
Consider

the demise of the river,
the fanged beast at the door of the sea.

It's a sentimental heart in a roomful of mirrors.
It's always an elegy.
Thinking of you, Dear,
                it's an elegy.

Elegy*

Cheran Rudhramoorthy

I have not seen
The first bird that spoke of spring
(Who has seen it?)

Nor have I seen the first leaf fall
That heralded the autumn
(Was it taken by the wind?
Or taken by the river?)

Yet
The emerging cold comes without warning
As the afternoon shrivels
And the time hastens when dusk falls.

As the waves sleep and the leaves change colour
On the shores of a lake devoid of birds
A sudden gust of wind
Denudes the trees

I asked a tree
That had turned its face from the water
And leaned away
Scratching the ground
With its long fingers:

What is this hatred of water?

---

* Translated from the Tamil by Nedra Rodrigo

This water is not like it was before
I am afraid
To see my reflection its face

The days when it glittered
Between
Deep blues and lush greens
Are lost

Even when the wind freezes in this great cold
The water refuses to freeze
Poison mingles in its essence

The creeping sea lotuses
That spread out their great leaves
For birds to walk on
Are destroyed

The golden fish, the star flower
And the long-legged turtle
Are devoured by salt

From this shore to that
The long, long heated pipes
Run below
Tearing through the body of the water
Cleaving icebergs
In the paths they create
The great ferries
Toil, heedless of day or night
Beneath the oily streaks they exude
The lake struggles for life

All is not as it was before

Uncertain, fearful
I turn to the earth again
There too the iceberg threatens
Says the tree

For nature, helpless and defeated
I write this elegy:

A great tree; a solitary tree; a tree alone.

Whiteness*

Abdul Hadi Sadoun

There are only poplars
river laughters
blue grass
. . . .
. . . .
And snow
. . . .
. . . .
Snow bales
sinking us into their threads.

Today, 29th November,
the city´s God
takes for breakfast drops of milk.

No one is on the streets,
a black spot in the distance
fading away.

No one is there,
Neither am I.

_____

* Translated from the Spanish by Manuel Neto Dos Santos

Diary of a Non-Essential Worker

Omar Sakr

Did you know violins can shake the earth? Such sweet vessels,
    tiny planetary throats. I was sent an orchestra. They made
    music, a sorrow, a soaring, that shivered the dirt.
I followed the notes to a barbarism. The composer said he
    created the beautiful hour
as a space to think about war, and I heard my mother's name,
    a dark cascade of her, I saw again the clamour behind her
    manner, her harrowed glamour; I am claiming all of it now
    not as a violence, but as an inevitability, always justifiable.
    I guess
I don't want to lose her, no matter the bruises. I haven't seen her
    in weeks, a memory of cherries, a perishable delight. I stay
    home, she stays home, and with this distance we become old
    battlefields, able to appreciate our damages without adding to
    them. How lucky we are to have homes. How likely it is we
    will lose them. Months ago we couldn't breathe and smoky
    miracles pulverised the sky, our fussy lungs.
Everything is a miracle when you are alive. I am learning that
    against my will. Today I was sent a pink dwarf kingfisher,
    a bird thought extinct for over a century, and still, it was
    someone's job to look for her, someone waited, camera in
    hand, for a glimpse of a glorious beak. Outside, I hear the
    camaraderie of ordinary wings, the chatter
of birds we call pests. They don't seem to mind the lockdown. I
    dare say they are having fun, a lark. I call my landlord, ask for
    a reprieve, and hear only birdsong.
He's having fun. I walk out into the park, where, months ago, a
    man was stabbed near to death; I sit on the bench close to

the stain his blood left and receive a text reminding me to
   care about Kashmir, and Gaza, and our Uyghur brothers and
   sisters, who I never stopped caring about, and for whom my
   care did nothing. Forgive me,
I sometimes mistake grief for care. The orchestra follows me
   under the foliage,
the violins unrelenting, the world shaken to their curvature, their
   high-strung demands, as I sift through the scattered lyric
   of my shattered life to find a way to love a woman, and the
   birds weave and whirl in the green, laughing at this non-
   essential work.

Waiting for News of Hurricane Dorian

Margaret R. Sáraco

I wake from unbalanced dreams
to the sound of healing bowl timbre
and logs neatly stacked by the hearth
highlighted by the morning sun.

Cicadas chirp rhythmically, even at dawn
breezes from the north rattle wind chimes,
and far away storms shake islands
in the Atlantic.

A lone can is kicked
rumbling down the street.
A hungry child wakes, then cries.
Reports arrive tempestuously
over airwaves with bad news.

Fire Reports

Igor Satanovsky

Russian Summer Fires of 2010

Dear xxxxx.
he was gone.
dreaming of.

a few months.
of Russian history.
air filters.

Dear xxxxx.
smoke poisoning.
were informed.

regarding the masks.
to get worse.
Consulate.

a few months.
smoke poisoning.
other pollutants.

Dear xxxxx.
will be informed.
chronic fatigue.

a few months ago.
age and health.

and health.

Dear xxxxx.
what a mess.
Consulate.

a few months.
and hospitalizations.
chronic fatigue.

Dear xxxxx.
he was already gone.
already gone.

Bushfires I (2019)

the pithecus curse
and australos on fire
the stink of smoked furs
floats over the mire

oh no piglet piglet
koala burns ganga
eeyore rabbit rabbit
roo roo kanga kanga

Bushfires II (2019)

ee no connecti
limate chang

iled to the bottom

umerous obit
olatile marke
iling fores

ility of cos
tensive operati
ectares lost

ied
uldn't say bette
and didn'

History*

K. Satchidanandan

History was there before us;
only, we were not there:
we, who believe we are witnesses to
the objects, plants and beasts on earth,
why, that they were all
created for us, even.

But they don't think so.
They were the witnesses to our emergence.
They blessed us,
gave us water and shade,
flowers, fruits, milk.

In the beginning we feared them,
and worshipped; then we
ousted them from history,
turned us into our slaves and menials.

Have you ever had to watch your brothers
being axed and sawn into pieces
to be sold in the timber market?
Or hanging on a hook, bleeding,
in the meat shop?

Our tribe doesn't have much time left.
Our own inventions will

---

* Translated from the Malayalam by the poet

render us redundant.
Those who saw our rise
will, in total detachment
watch our fall.

They will survive,
to write a new history where
the tale of our arrival and departure
will be told in just a paragraph,
scribbled on brown rocks and green leaves,
by the liquid fingers of the rain
falling from the sapphire clouds,
in the secret language of the leaf-veins
and the tortoise-shell:
the minute history of the universe
caught by their own meticulous antennae,
where only they will feature,
and their God.

Emily Brontë's Advice for the Anthropocene*

Jane Satterfield

'Hers is a Green and animal beyond . . .'
—Stevie Davies, Emily Brontë

Enjoy every sandwich? Haworth was a maze
of multiplying middens, mills, the pumped-up
clouds of industry, heathered moors a haven in
a century's shrinking space. Tempting, yes,
to stick to chores, scrub the parlour carpet,
remain, in fact, remote. But as the saying goes,
there is no later. This is later—arctic ice melts,
shears off, strange carvings stun the circumspect
to speech. If Emily were here today,
what would she say? Though twilight calls
for a generous pour, it's better to learn dark
sonatas, the heart's own haul of grief.
The soul's compass is—or ought to be—
set straight for the storm. Some species
die without a fellow creature's comfort—
sparrows sometimes fail to thrive when solitary.
The auk's line, I've read, unraveled when stumblers
dropped the eggs. Troubadours enshrine
the human truths—lies, betrayals, love
gone astray. What else would she tell us?
Aim to take dictation—a rabbit
grooming in the grass calls down the watchful hawk,
the robin's clutch in turn attracts the foraging crow.

---

* First appeared in *Interim*

And would we listen to her counsel
as we stand stoic in the bracing air, embrace
the static stare of endlings? Look up, she'd say,
you will come to call them kin.

The Question*

Jane Schapiro

Have you ever stood on the edge of a shore looked at the sea
    absorbed
in your worried thoughts
not really seeing the sea even though your eyes are fixed on the
    water
but you're swimming in your own pool
feeling anxious bored thinking maybe you'll leave get a drink
when suddenly in the distance
you catch a glimmer of something you're not sure what
so you keep watching looking
really looking and then you see it and you're sure that glint
is a fin breaking through
rising vanishing rising and you can't take your eyes off the sea
you're staring ahead
so focused so absorbed in the water the air the creature
that you wait through
heat thirst restlessness for a flash of life entering light
blowing out spray
before it descends and you are grateful to be present
absorbed in that moment
when air sea fin merge in a synchronicity of wholeness
a moment of why.

---

* From *Let The Wind Push Us Across*, Antrim House, 2017

Plate Histrionics

Larissa Shmailo

He throws a gold-lamé wedding-set saucer
    at me, and spits, 'There is no
        global warm-ing.'

      Today, Irma evacuates Sarasota as b-
    rother Harvey peers and jeers, Ozymandiu-
s-like, Houston and Florida, look upon me.

A-s th-ese li-nes are bro-ken, so the dream-
    s of cities, and those hamlets and towns a-
      way where we settled to breathe, hear our-
        selves think.

      Cat 5, there is no stronger. An
evil fidget spinner, Irma swirls out of a wet
hell, and I holler CLIMATE CHANGE.

It is the
    imitation
        Wedgewood gravy boat, h-
            e throws that next, jjjjjjjust before she

Everyday Mishap*

Shafi Shauq

In the tree near the window of the 12-storey apartment,
A thrush sings full throated its spring-song;
The eyelids are dry after the nightly mayhem of dreams,
Dew might soothe them; morning shine is on the cliffs.

On the top-branch is perched a thrush, gives out a call:
All frontiers of war are silenced, truce is proclaimed;
The six dimensions are replete with seven-note symphony,
Expressionless songs surge out and seek vent to flow.

Now all the discordant loudspeakers of the city resound,
Hoarse and phlegm-filled throats raise a din of prayers:
'Forgive our sins! Let our profits swell! Be our daughters safe!'
A spate of mud and sediment surges to bury the lotuses.

Today also, like other days, a wall caves in upon me,
The thrush is lost, and I too am lost until the evening.

---

* *Translated from the Kashmiri by the poet*

Roads and Paths Covered; Flash Flooding on Steeper Slopes

Clare Shaw

The air is forest.
The road is blocked with trees.
There is noise between them
and no word except *river*;
the canal is fast river; the path
is deep river; the river is a story
that can't be believed.

The birds have all left the woods.
The lane is a ripped-up book.
And as much as you know of rain—
this rain is taking everything.
Your clothes forget themselves,
your shoes have never been dry.

It has drowned the rabbits.
They could not escape
from the cage where you kept them.
It is lifting the hens in their coop—
you can still hear them scream.
It breaks your phone

and the lights.
You are left in the total dark.

When your town is a river
and everywhere you love
is going under;

when even the boats can't float
and the water is at your door and rising,
when the mice have all fled upstairs;

when no-one can reach you,
the only choice you can make
is what you can lift and save,
is not to forget you can leave -
is to wade with the weight of a child on your shoulders,
to follow instructions for crossing deep water
though the current grows steadily stronger and deeper.

Your house is a river.
Now swim.

O Water-diviner!

H.S. Shivaprakash

O water-diviner! O water-diviner!
Show me where is the wellspring,
The wet eye of earth's core,
The compassion of clouds and rocks

Coco water Limca water
Water imprisoned in bottles
Water enchanted by sly
Magicians of market
Sweat-water blood-water-
Drunken on all these waters
My tongue has turned a burning shard
Fires are raging in the heart
Famine is spreading in the guts

Auctioned rivers are crying out
O water-diviner! O water-diviner!
Dying oceans are crying out
O water-diviner! O water-diviner
Wells full of corpses are crying out
O water-diviner! O water-diviner
No end to the cry of ponds
O water-diviner! O water-diviner
Ponds and wells, rivers and oceans
Are crying out in a chorus
O water-diviner! O water-diviner
No more coolness in our water
No strength to quench thirst

Tell us where is the wellspring
The spring of sweet cooling water
That can quench all our thirst

In the midst of day's endless labor
And, at night, catching fire
Like will-o-the wisp
Beings of our secret dreams
Are constantly crying out
In every human tongue
In every cry of every beast
And in silences
Of destroyed crops
And lifeless things:
O water-diviner! O water-diviner
Wake up your sleeping wand
Turn it towards the wellspring
O when will you tell all of us
Look! Here it is!
The panacea for all ills
The life-giving gurgling water
Here it is! Right here!

O water-diviner! O water-diviner

(Crete, 7.2.2018)

Wasp*

Penelope Shuttle

Thanks to global warming
an Inuit community
up in the Arctic Circle
sees its first ever wasp

But they have no word
for wasp
and obey local radio warnings
not to touch the creature

which has no word
in wasp for ice
any more than a Japanese sex doll
has a word for love

---

* *Wasp* was first published in my pamphlet *Four Portions of everything on the menu for M'sieur Monet!'*, Indigo Dreams Publications, 2016.

Hawk

Laura Shovan

It is young, unsleek, feathers puffed against cold.
It stands to one side of the swing set's beam,
talons deep in last night's snow.

The children and I crowd the back door,
take turns with binoculars meant for star gazing.
They get bored, return to breakfast

while I look and look. The bird's eyes
are goofy with surprise. It can't figure out
how it came to our yard, why it's perched on—

of all things—a swing set. It stares at our house
as if it knew this place once.
It looks confused, the way we all get confused,

finding ourselves in an undignified moment,
perched on a dilapidated swing set
or squashed—as I was, just last night—

under a pile of laughing, near-grown children.
The hawk raises one yellow claw
places it deep in snow, swoops away.

The kids pack for school. Binoculars in their case.
When I stop and hold still, I get a little dizzy
from the suddenness of it.

The Unreadable Dictionaries of Our Actions

Ndaba Sibanda

We are the idioms of our time, our sphere
for we belong to the same era, ecosphere,
yet, we are like measly words whose ovaries
and gist no soul can establish from the glossaries
of our shady actions. A life whose paths lead to ruin
as the world struggles with floods or lack of rain.

Our consumption patterns, our careless lifestyles,
our previous actions and decisions are our dirty files
that should be our proverbs for posterity and stability
yet we fail to infer from the lessons of our stupidity,
from wise sayings. A life whose paths lead to ruin
as the world struggles with floods or lack of rain.

Home

Sean Singer

Sing-start. More of a wide
rich-tree-cube. Floral oil.
Silver salve-tin. Hat-moat
on the bottom of a shingle.

Loss is still *ours*, and I swirl down
a euphonium, the shape of a kingdom.
I get smaller through loss, circles. figureheads
sobbing hillsides, fire figure, curve-hover.

I left the rim of the instrument—a wide leaf—
refilled, a light moth,
amber green, wing-horn, feeler . . .
ear-heart, inside a wreath.

Memories of an Asbestos Village

Ari Sitas

When I was a dustman scraping at asbestos rock
I learnt well the meaning of a landslide and the meaning
of airborne fibre.
Their stealth, well-rhymed with death.

The slide would shred your skin against the roughage
sharp edges would slice a shortcut to your sirloin
Airborne fibre, that soft whisper and glide would
turn your lung to crimson, then ash
Through both, death would hover
like an ocelot stalking, searching for the knocker

Eggheads would come to look for rickets or bacteria
measure the remnants of your karma, stethoscopes would
        measure your
contract days, forceps would yank out some soul-piece.

I was saved by a landslide, however severe the cuts
My windpipe is a strainer of what rocks and what rolls
and what exhales like wheezing, the peppery saliva has not left me,
new moons bring back the taste of overcooked goat
by the fullness of moon it all turns acrid

What's left for me
In the shadow of the abandoned mountain
is to clean the watercourse
to the village
as if someone will return to ring

the school's bell
perchance to look for water:
the village waits in patience
its dried out marina,
its fishbone, the dark skeletons of burnt-out tractors
and ocean craft its residue of bygone wealth
its empty graveyard whose marble stones were pilfered.

Papine

Malachi Smith

Zoop, zop, zoop
Zoop, zoop, zoop
Zoop, zoop, zoop
La la la la la
La la la la la

Celebrating a Jamaican spring morning
Kool FM dishing sweet soul melodies
antioxidants eliminating
free radicals from the stream.

Constant Spring rises in the distance
like flute notes
starburst sunrays sweep my gaze.

Her green roof stretched
can't cover the fire rust
zinc fences of her neighbors.

Gully banks stripped of their identity
nothing grows now
not even the living dead
who refuses to move to higher ground.

A minibus of noises invades my solitude
bad man tunes rapid firing

beautiful people packed like sardines
can't breathe.

They see ugly, feel ugly
hear ugly, hoping
the next stop is Papine;
living dead stay silent while
the noise a buss up them head.

Tired of hearing the same old
wash up Cartel and gully bank stuff
they wrap, sell, feed, inject
into conscious, subconscious cognitive centers.

Want to hear rain tongue
licking zinc roof belly clean
finding grooves tracing
igniting lightning thunder streams
of warmth that only rain God
tongue fingers can feel.

Want to see a dragonfly
kissing a rainbow angel
high up over a blooming poinsettia
as psychedelic as a Marley spliff pull
on a mystic morning.

Turn down the noise
increase the positive vibes
on this tropical soft lit morning

want to hear waves lashing
bashing, crashing, caressing screaming
across Robin's Bay mouth
melodies of love and happiness.

I turn up my stereo
and down struck the distraction

This Thread that Holds It All Up

Rafel Soler

From clover its buttonholes
and from bread its jubilation

from yellow fruit its darkest rind
from the others their hapless suit
headed for the gullet

from the bird its fit of flutter
from flight its foretaste
from desert strewn tablecloths

from the knife
the seams it causes

from the book that I am not writing
the story that is not of its own

from hunger don't even name it

from the blind and large tree
its root like a flag

and from a solemn sea
nothing.

Plastic Plasma Paradox

Mark Spitzer

.

we wake up in beds
made of plastic
get dressed in clothes
spun from plastics
open shades
plastic plastic
make breakfast with
plasticware
in walls full of plastic
on floors packed with plastic
then drive to work
in vehicles assembled
from hundreds of plastics
our phones forged
from plastics
plastic shoes
plastic hats
plastic glasses
plasti-products
on our faces
in our hair
in our teeth
in our bones
in our blood
typing on computers
fused with plastic
eating lunch

wrapped in plastic
served on plastic
plastic straws
and utensils
before going home
to plastic appliances
and more plastic screens
and plastic machines
for climate control
plastic fixtures beaming light
soaking up
plastic dust
diffused through
PVC
only to end up
with plastic tubes
up our noses
and down our throats
waiting for a plastic bag
to take us to a plastic casket
made with plastic paint
and plastic glue
Holy Poly-
Urethane You!

And we wonder why
we're all dying
from what we're all
dying from.

Climb the Tallest Poem You Can Dream

K. Srilata

Climb the tallest poem you can dream—
that's the only way to find them,
mildly rebellious siblings
lined up in a row and shot dead
on the forest floor, on city roads,
their branches inter-locked arms.

Climb the tallest poem you can dream—
that's the only way to find them,
these tree poems the earth wrote us,
their death the heavy-wood-grief
of doors slammed, one by one by one
on your life, on mine.

Idiot's Guide to Counting*

Margo Taft Stever

How do you become one
with the horse, riding and becoming
the act of riding,
and the horse becoming the self
and the other at exactly
the same second, counting strides,
counting muscle movement,
counting fences, hurtling over
them with the horse, counting
the everything
of one?

How do you count, how do you
pull a muscle turning over
in bed at night—measurements
that change everything, counting
back to everything, the everything
of one, the pulled muscles of the back
of one, the entanglement
of one, the waves of particles
counting back, the quantum?

---

* First published in *Blackbird*. Also, published in *The Lunatic Ball*, Margo Taft Stever, Kattywompus Press, 2015, in *Cracked Piano*, Margo Taft Stever, CavanKerry Press, 2019, in *enskyment Online Anthology of Poetry*, edited by Dan Masterson, enskyment.org., 2018, and in *Reflecting Pool: Poets and the Creative Process*, edited by Laurance Carr, Codhill Press, 2018)

How to become one with
the branches of a tree, a grandfather
tree in an apple orchard
that no longer exists?
Separate one
from tree, horse,
counting numbers, counting
the grandfather tree
to find the solution of
one.

Counting trees, leaves, counting
everything as no longer
existing, counting
trees as one with the everything
that no longer exists.

Song of the Lion's Son
(For Benjamin Gerbi)

Toni Giselle Stuart

there is a call that comes silent
as Lion's track on the trail,
soft as the silhouette of a dugout at dusk,
sharp as the sting of Kalahari sand, yet
true as the necked embrace of Zebras.
when it finds you, you are returned
to the place your heart grows still
and there, under new moon sky,
the silver stars sing around your feet
at the fire. an old man looks up
in greeting. you say hello, reach out
your hand. he smiles, then points to the sand,
and with a stick begins to draw.
he does not speak, but his voice rings
through the dark quiet of the trees,
long before the two-legged became two-legged
he was Baobab and Kwagga. his breath was
south-easter and Eagle's cry, reaching
across the open plains: he was freedom.
the old man's voice descends your spine,
when the two-legged first became two-legged
he remembered that he was once Bontebok
and Wildebeest, that his heart was once
Sugarbird's wing and his eyes were once
grains of sand, walked upon by hoof and paw

but the longer the two-legged walked on two legs,
he began to forget. first he forgot he was the dew
at dawn. then he forgot he was the wild rush
of waterfall and sea. then he forgot the Leopard
was his father, and the Swallow was his sister.

a slow sadness creeped into the two-legged's heart
and he walked out of the veld, the bush,
the forest, the desert. so the first mother and
the first father, created a song, delicate
as Spider's web, yet just as strong. a song
to reach through the two-legged's forgetting
and bring him home. he may not remember but
he would return, to the place his heart grew still.
the old man looks up to meet your eyes.
he smiles, welcome home, Lion's son.

Ark-Shaped Plus Neck

Terese Svoboda

She walks the shore, kempt and clipped,
just-so wings, a lion's glance across

the blue savannah, no sand gritting her double lids,
her etcetera's a dance of known nouns vs.

the lapping of perception: an oceanimity.
Really, the bird's Sphinx-mysterious,

female by stripes, fallen from a cloud the size
of a house now laddering the sky

with V's in proportion,
dangling legs probably painful from walking.

I want wings rings the rest of creation, *let us
ream gravity.* Here at my feet,

six more reckon the water with their stares,
absorbing the adjectives of another exit.

Safe on land, on sea and air,
fewer survive each year.

Canadian Geese: Then and Now

Katherine Barrett Swett

Then honking passed
    and silence followed,
        winter emptiness
    swallowed

the raucous fall
    of fruitfulness,
        but now their call
  is seasonless.

    The gorgeous sound
      of flying Vs
    now circles down
  to hiss at me.

    The melancholy
  sticks around
and drops its feces
    on the ground.

Lost sign of fall
    and turning leaves,
      the hollow call
        now never leaves.

Water

George Szirtes

The hard beautiful rules of water are these:
That it shall rise with displacement as a man
does not, nor his family. That it shall have no plan
or subterfuge. That in the cold, it shall freeze;
in the heat, turn to steam. That it shall carry disease
and bright brilliant fish in river and ocean.
That it shall roar or meander through metropolitan
districts whilst reflecting skies, buildings and trees.

And it shall clean and refresh us even as we slave
over stone tubs or cower in a shelter or run
into the arms of a loved one in some desperate quarter
where the rats too are running. That it shall have
dominion. That it shall arch its back in the sun
only according to the hard rules of water.

At Seneca Creek in the Fall

Marianne Szlyk

Brown leaves drift down like birds,
land on the creek, float away.

Turtles, like hard brown leaves,
drift above the creek floor.

Yellow leaves dazzle,
sunlight on a cloudy day.

In the clearing, mosquitos rise.
Last bees browse on goldenrod

that floods the field.

A tree stoops to take a drink
from the dry pond.

Mushrooms spring up on fallen trees—
were they always there?

The Proud Man*

Bei Ta

People tell him
That the would-be journey
Has all been arranged
That all turning points
Have been marked
And all rupturing points
Have bridges
Following the sun
He will have a huge shadow
And distinctive seasons

The proud man
Prefers to cover his own eyes
With a black cloth
He knows that there's little difference
Between the scenes far away
And objects nearby
He will make completely new observations and judgments
With his own soul about all things

The proud man
Has taken away the temple's keys
Disciples have nowhere to worship
The proud man
Has taken away the piano's tones
Audiences have their ears deafened

---

* *Translated from the Chinese by the poet with Ken Parson*

The proud man
Has taken away the ordinary ways
Travelers lost their legs
He needs no homestead
To stop his wandering
He needs no seasons
To change his clothes
He needs no stars

The proud man
Has passed one and another field
And abandoned one and another village
All the way, the flood surging
And beasts manifolding
The proud man
Away from all the others
The mounts have been lowering
In his climbing
He cut off one and another section
Of the ladder of success
And broke one and another
Ancient monument
The proud man
Forged of thorns and stones
Yet makes thorns blossom
And stones smooth
The clear font irrigates his body
So that all lives flourish
The proud man
Is a fertile land when he lies down

View from a Shiva Shrine

Anand Thakore

Elephant Bathing

He will never go there again,
Hip-flask in pocket, camera at hand,
Far from the crowded confines
Of the human animal he could not trust,
To the lush cricket-choired thickets
He so jealously loved;
Dense, creeper-canopied spaces
Where he would listen eagerly
For the sudden slither of a python's tail,
Or the persistent mating calls of leopard and crane,
Studying the stealthy ways of predator and prey,
Till panther, bison, hyena and stag
Seemed part of a single guileless continuum
He had only begun to see his part in.
Now home and city hunt him down,
Building about him their busy labyrinth
Of doctors, nurses, brothers and sons;
Though tiger and spotted deer remain,
Frozen above his bed in black and white.
An egret pecks noiselessly at a crocodile's jaws,
As pale flamingoes, stripped irretrievably of their pinks,
Leap into a flight forever deferred.
Where you are going, they seem to say,
You will have no need for us or all you remember.
And yet the thought of getting there is not unlike
A great lone tusker taking the plunge,

His vast grey bulk sinking below the riverline
Against a clear black sky,
Till there is no more of him to see
Than a single tusk,
White as a quarter-moon in mid-July,
Before the coming of a cloud.

From 'Shapeshifter'

Jeet Thayil

How to Be a Leaf

Hold your breath until
you are God's green thoughts.
Stop eating.

air will suffice for food
Water is another matter:
The skin absorbs moisture,

Eyes adjust
limbs grow inward
Conjugate patience.

Worship women and trees.

How to Be a Horse

Know the nostril,
all power gathers there.
Inflate yours until the blood sings.

You will need all your training
to be horse, not ass.
It is a thin crossing

Perilous to the absent-minded
and estranged of heart.
Avoid all latitudes.

How to be A Crow

Learn to name animals
-Stinking, Babbling, Breedy,
Querulous, Maddened, and Jet.

Usurp the duties of God.
Why not?
This is what poets do.

As for crow,
kill colour,
turn black.

How to Be a Bandicoot

Assume dominance
over the underworld.
Your enemies are legion

-eat them.
Eat everything.
You must build your strength,

change will surely come.
Your eyes are red legends.
Your name is Adam.

How to be a Krait

This one is easy,
let your grief take over.
Enjoy salt.

Forget the rest.
When your skin falls off
sere as bone,

laugh out loud.
That is the first thing. The second:
Avoid the mongoose.

Expectantly . . .

A.J. Thomas

An overcast sky
A strong cold north wind blowing down from the Mediterranean—
Heading north along a happy go lucky road
At 180 kilometres an hour
The turmeric terrain of the upper Sahara
Punctuated with stunted olives, eucalyptus
And lesser smudges of dark green—
Straggling shrubs hopeful to make it
To the future.
Small flocks of sheep
And a precious goat;
Road-signs with the picture
Of a camel.
But what's here!
The intermittent tattered patches of green
Grass sprouting at first rain
Expectantly
As if they were waiting with bated breath
To be tapped on the head by pit-pat raindrops
Calling out to them, 'rise!'

The Guest Worker's Daughter*

Alexei Tsvetkov

birds are singing in a foreign language
we don't listen unless spoken to directly
trees grow up just fine in spite of
being unloved by their parents
trees do not sing nor do birds bear
fruit in the usual sense but there's still
more likeness between them and them
than between them and us
they have resigned themselves to this difference
which we interpret to our own advantage

the teacher lady is speaking to us
she is speaking in an unknown language
we are unknown children we were schooled
in a classroom at the edge of the last continent
the teacher lady is faking an interest
in what we will grow up to become
it would be strange if she asked the trees
the same question but no one has thought of it

as the continent is about to expire we see
a light addressed to those trees in the window
which is not the same light as that
which was prescribed for us
birds are singing in a foreign language

---
* Translated from the Russian by Philip Nikolayev

because any language is foreign
compared to all the others

the lowest achieving girl in the classroom
secretly knows she'll grow up to become
none other than what she already is of herself
but it is reprehensible to publicly admit it
and she has already been referred to the birds
in terms of not being the brightest of the flock
and asked if she wasn't a guest worker's daughter

human children in the classroom
are learning how not to think of the season
when they will turn into swifts and mulberries
and when the teacher lady's phony question
will pose itself again in an unforeseen context
only foreseeable contexts are safe to face
they lied to us that this wasn't the last continent
we failed to notice that this light belonged to others

The Horse Flew Above*

Anubhav Tulasi

The tanga was light as the wind
The horse was nimbler than the wind
As the wheels and axel hubs of the tanga moved on
The stars revolved in their high spirits
With the clattering music of the horse's hoofs
The planets evolved in their high spirits

The tanga was a giant stone
Without wheels and axel hubs
A single horse could not draw it
He collapsed while trying

One day the tanga really changed into the wind
Another day water-like the tanga flowed into the river
It sank trying to drift like a boat
One day the horse really turned into the wind
Yet another day the horse got watery wings
Vaporous the horse left for another planet

The *tangawala* changed into a still tree
That very day the tree was cut down
A forest taller than the trees sprang up
Such a forest engulfed the earth

It's a modern tale of the sun changing over from
The horse drawn tanga to another vehicle

---

* Translated from the Assamese by Nirendra Nath Thakuria

Dalim O Dalim what have you brought for us
I've brought I've brought the lost horse
Put the bell on the neck

Maitri

Annakutty Valiamangalam

Day and night you stand as a guardian angel
in the centre of my garden, small.
The green leaves whispering the holy Mantra
to the breeze—of *Maitri*,
audible to the ears, visible to the eyes
through the windows of my house
You my friend the ancient Banyan Tree
Silence, perseverance, strength
and kindness, you freely teach me!
Like a *Brahmavihara*, open for all
sheltering the birds, the bats, the monkeys,
the termites, ants and insects of all sorts
shedding shadows and cool air
to those searching humans,
weary of the scorching sun.
The peacocks glide in at times
on cloudy days at your feet
and pay homage with their dance!
Your tender roots—peep down into the air
searching the earth below—or perhaps
stretching your hands to embrace
the Mother Earth to give her solace!
Your unconditional friendship
Maitri puts me to shame!
without judgemental looks and acts
accepting everything, every living being.
The sunshine, the moon smiling,
the tears pouring from the skies,

the gentle wind and the storm alike
all the moods of *Prakrti* you witness
in solemn Silence!
Your boundless kindness and compassion
towards all alike without any discrimination
Abide in Loving Kindness!
that mode of Existence yours
You teach us every moment
in Sacred Silence and remind us
of the Holy Emptiness of Existence
revealed once to Siddhartha—the prince,
transforming him to the Awakened One!

O my Friend the Bodhi Tree
we are waiting for another Buddha
to save our Planet from destruction!
to share and care for all,
initiate us humans into that
Loving Kindness that would
save the whole planet Earth!
with all its species endangered
rainforests disappearing
with its suffering migrant folk!
Lead us to the mystery of
that all embracing Maitri!
Fratelli Tutti!

Rain, Wind

Veerankutty

Every rain
is an ocean overturned.
Who is it that dries it up
when God's ships
fail to reach the earth?

Wind is cotton
soaked in ether
that God
drops down.
Will it have ways left
to travel back
carrying the pain
from the wounds?

Pachyderm Refugee

Pramila Venkateswaran

There she lay, a boulder, panting, in a muddy pool,
a large tear on her wrinkled posterior opening smooth pink flesh.

Don't look away, as the men, dhotis rolled up their thighs,
bathe her, intoning '*Irayana, Irayana*,' soothing her.

Bow your head, as you did at the temple when she blessed you
with her trunk. You did not see her legs and torso cut by chains

tying her to the floor of a temple stall. Weep, as the men hose
     her
gray skin flapping open like a door to reveal the wound.

You wince as their brushes rub her obedient body stuck
in torture's groove. Her fan-like ears had received her kin's cries,

now are calmed with ointments, therapies embroidering her with
     balms
to reverse years of abuse in devout dens scented with incense.

Her knees are reverse L-shaped as she offers herself to treatment.
Heavy with grief, you kneel, your palms pressed together.

Imagining a Dystopian Future

Marc Vincenz

Doubtlessly dying, a lone rock is imagined in space,
A collection of words, an uplifting truth in the serum,

In the biological cocktail. Slight shift and every-
Thing changes. The locals so quiet in the pub, simply

Sipping their rum and cokes, the Spanish blue fades
To continental gray. External moments are imagined

more than lived ad infinitum. Get your arse
out here, Uncle Rahul would say in his crisp

white suit, suiting himself to my Auntie Fatima.
And all the Christmas cards thrown away,

The hundred images of folklore and mythology,
The pyres and effigies burning, the fumes

Obscuring the evening of its scented candles and
Cheap perfume. *Wash your feet*, the naked man

Covered in a beard says.
Everywhere you walk you casts dirty shadows.

The black hole is doubtlessly sleeping.
Only its back is visible.

Place*

Heidi Williamson

When we left, we left it all:
the hazel, the spruce, the Scots pine, the aspen.

When we left we took it all:
the skyscapes and treescapes framing each season.

When we left, we left it all:
the bracken, the cabins, the pathways of water.

When we left we took it all:
the hollows, chill soil, ice-air and snowfall.

When we left, we left it all:
angular boulders with ashy thin grasses.

When we left we took it all:
scent of just-rained-on expanding the stonework.

When we left, we left it all:
pine martens, red deer, herons and osprey.

When we left we took it all:
broadening clouds blending with hillsides.

---

* From *Return by Minor Road*, Bloodaxe, 2020

When we left, we left it all:
short-lived supple islands of shingle.

When we left we took it all:
the bend in the loch we can't see beyond.

Trees*
Jerusalem

Michele Wolf

The spade hits a stone. And the stone, asleep
In this spot for centuries, will not be moved.
So, I carry the two baby shoots, cupping
Each by its bundle of roots, a few feet away,
Then dig in a softer place, where the dirt
And smaller stones give easily. Gathering
The graveled soil with my hands, tamping
It down, I set these trees into the earth,
The home where I put you, Father, and put
You, Sister. I plant two-foot-high cypresses
In your names, gardening a barren
Hill in the family plot, the land of Abraham.

They join acres of forests planted tree by tree,
Until 200 million were planted, and a people
Who reclaimed a desert, their hands in the soil.
How much wandering, and how many stones
In the path, before we can stand on the land
We were promised, before we succumb to the land
As stones ourselves. Yet stands of our trees,
Limbs shifting in the breeze, keep on breathing.
I plant trees among stones, and after I leave,

---

* *Trees* has previously appeared in *Conversations During Sleep* by Michele Wolf © 1998, published by Anhinga Press and winner of the Anhinga Prize for Poetry. *Trees* also received an Anna Davidson Rosenberg Award.

Each raises its dusty face to feed on the sunlight,
To exhale what's unseen, the element that gives
Us the chance to wake and dance, and grieve.

A Natural History of the United States

Sam Wronoski

Primarily there were rocks,
the silicates: quartz, (we'll list them),
feldspars—orthoclase locked
in pegmatites made up a vast expanse,
trace elements: copper, nickel,
twisted knobs of gold in hematite.
Obviously, there was water.
For example, observe the canyons,
large salt deposits, clear evidence
of glacial scour, puddingstone.
Scurrying over it, arthropods
turkeys, ammonites, everything
that crawls or swims, the inland
seas teeming with jellyfish
obtuse things with pulsing notochords,
angry primates filled with ecstasy.
Beneath them concrete slabs, long bridges,
chewing gum. The wheels that crush things
churning, monuments on hill tops,
a single tractor trailer sitting idle
thrummed like a cicada once.
In other words, the stage was set for us
to pin up maps around the living room.

Outside the Window of Bertolt Brecht's Former Residence*

Gong Xuan

Autumn is hidden behind a white house
Beyond its closed window, a tree
Covers up the melancholy of Dorotea cemetery

The falling leaves are obsessed with the sighing winds.
There is none other than silence
That cares about the lonely gravestones here

Look the other way: you will see his profile,
His gestures, old vets,
A scroll painting of Confucius, a bronze statue of Lao Tseu
On a donkey, the philosopher's fancies.

I came here with no illusions, no hope of wealth,
He is sleeping. His dream has no shadows.
His genius knows the seeds of justice will surely sprout.

Light silently falls on the house; weeds, their heads held high
Record for the world the bygone beauty, the living kindness.

Once you said truth is time's child. When daisies blossom
There won't be any more moral lessons in Three-penny Opera.
You, like me, will just see the patient sunshine, trees, flowers
And all the love that fills the world

---

* Translated from the Chinese by Bei Ta with K. Satchidanandan

I Fear a Shapeless Knife*

Tian Xiang

I was raised by the river
I will return to it in the end.

The river will ever be singing in my body
To the very end of my life.

My father died when the river in him dried up,
And so am I predestined to die.

I listen carefully to the river, and talk to it
I am infatuated with its endless water and
The divine light playing on its waves.

It brings me joy, washes away my solitude and humiliation
Yet, like time, like wind, it will rob me of my life too.
The moment they give, they also begin to demand
But I accept my fate; and lead my life afraid of a shapeless knife.

I will follow the river's call; I have nowhere else to go.

---

* Translated from the Chinese by Bei Ta with K. Satchidanandan

Climate Change

Anton Yakovlev

The sublime, sanctified snow scrubber
from the Stop & Shop where you briefly worked
cleans my car so nicely after the storms.

You work a full-time job developing memes
to combat global warming deniers.

I hear the ocean currents
will shift as the planet warms
and winters will grow only
colder in this part of the country.

Everytime I brush the snow off my car,
another plastic thread falls out of the brush.

I gather them the way I used to
gather the loose hairs on the floor
after massaging your head.

An Overslept Flower*

Yang Yang Yujun

They all came out in January,
Covering the whole fence

Some faded in February
Like firecrackers set off

Only a green curtain was left in March
Dotted with yellow leaves

Between March and April a flower came,
A surprise, dreamy, like an overslept girl

It brought a message: Pyrostegia Venusta
Is a fuming volcano too.

---

* Translated from the Chinese by Bei Ta

Women of the Fields

Andrena Zawinski

'That's the history of the world. His story is told, hers isn't.'
—Dolores Hueta

The women of the fields clip red bunches of grapes
in patches off neatly tilled farmland in the San Joaquin,
clip sweet globes they can no longer stand to taste.
Just twenty miles shy of Santa Cruz beach babies in thongs,
Pleasure Beach surfers on longboards, all the cool convertibles
speeding Cabrillo Highway, women line as pickers—
back bent over another summer's harvest.

The campesinas labor without shade tents or water buffalos,
shrouded in oversized shirts and baggie work pants, disguised
as what they are not, faces masked in bandanas under cowboy hats
in fils de calzón:

> The young one named Ester taken in the onion patch
> with the field boss' gardening shears at her throat.
> The older one called Felicia isolated in the almond orchard
> and pushed down into a doghouse. The pretty one, Linda,
> without work papers, asked to bear a son in trade
> for a room and job in the pumpkin patch, Isabel, ravaged
> napping under a tree at the end of a dream after a long
> day picking pomegranates, violación de un sueño
> Salomé on the apple ranch forced up against the fence
> as the boss bellowed ¡Dios mío! to her every no, no, no.

The promotoras flex muscle in words, steal off into night
face-to-face to talk health care, pesticides, heatstroke, rape,
meet tally accounts—forced to exchange panties for paychecks
in orchards, on ranches, in fields, in truck beds—to speak out
to risk joblessness or deportation to an old country, a foreign soil.

Women of the fields, like those before them, like those
who will trail after—las Chinas, Japonesas, Filipinas—
to slave for frozen food empires in pesticide drift,
residue crawling along skin, creeping into nostrils
and pregnancies it ends as they hide from La Migra
in vines soaked in toxins or crawl through sewer tunnels,
across railroad tracks, through fences to pick our sweet berries,
for this, this: la fruta del diablo.

I Travel to a Lonely Island

Eva Christina Zeller

The stones flinch though untouched
And the wind is not to be brought from his rage
It goes straight through me

The heather sighs at my step
It's the dead they say here
I light candles and the wood in the stove
I apologise with an exacting gaze

The spiders are marked with death's heads
The snakes with yellow collars
The seagull is alert
The swallow chicks look down on me

I wash my hands in the cold sea
I bow to the wind

Cooing*

William Zhou (Zhou Se-se)

I hear my hometown cooing in my head
The ponds are cooing, the dried leaves, the pumpkin fields.
But not the frog: it crouches in the field, paranoiac,
Its round eyes stiffened.
Nor the boy lying on the plank:
He is playing a death-game: As soon as I go near,
He is sure to leap up and push me down.

---

* *Translated from the Chinese by Bei Ta with K. Satchidanandan*

References

1. Illich, Ivan. *Tools for Conviviality.* New York: Harper and Row, 1973.
2. Descartes, René, 1596-1650. *Discourse on Method.* New York : London: Macmillan ; Collier Macmillan, 1986.
3. Rees, Graham, ed. *The Oxford Francis Bacon Volume Xi: The Instauratio Magna Part Ii: Novum Organum and Associated Texts.* Clarendon Press, 2004.
4. Smith, Adam. *Wealth of Nations.* Wordsworth Editions, 2012.
5. Ponting, Clive. *A Green History of the World: The Environment and the Collapse of Great Civilizations.* Penguin Books, 1992.
6. Fischer, Ernst, Translated, Bostock, Anna. *The Necessity of Art: A Marxist Approach.* London: Verso, 2010.
7. Horkheimer, Max and Adorno, W. Theodor. *Dialectic of Enlightenment: Philosophical Fragments.* Amsterdam: Querido, 1947, and California: Stanford University Press, 2002.
8. Pepper, David. Eco-Socialism: From Deep Ecology to Social Justice. London and New York: Routledge, 1993.
9. Rueckert, William. *Literature and Ecology: An Experiment in Eco-Critiism,* 1978.
10. Meeker, Joseph. The Comedy of Survival: Studies in Literary Ecology. Scribner,1974.
11. Glotfelty, Cheryll and Fromm, Harold. *The Ecocritical Reader:* Landmarks in Literary Ecology. The University of Georgia Press, 1996.
12. Buell, Lawrence. The Future of Environmental Criticism. Oxford: Blackwell, 2005.

13. Birkerts, Sven. *Only God can Make a Tree: The Joys and Sorrows of Eco-Criticism.* Boston Book Review 3/1, 1996.
14. Said, Edward. *Humanism and Democratic Criticism. New York:* Columbia University Press, 2004.
15. Zizek, Slavov. *Nature and its Discontents.* Vol. 37, No. 3, Issue 117: The Political Animal, pp. 37-72. Baltimore: The Johns Hopkins University Press, 2008.

About the poets of *Greening the Earth*

Abhay K. is the author of nine poetry collections and the editor of *The Bloomsbury Book of Great Indian Love Poems* (2018), *CAPITALS* (2017), *The Bloomsbury Anthology of Great Indian Poems* (2019) and *New Brazilian Poems* (2019). He received the SAARC Literary Award 2013 and was invited to record his poems at the Library of Congress, Washington DC in 2018.

Shanta Acharya is the author of twelve books; her latest publications include *What Survives Is the Singing* (2020) and *Imagine: New and Selected Poems* (2017).

Usha Akella has authored four books of poetry, one chapbook and scripted and produced one musical drama. She recently earned a master's degree in creative writing from Cambridge University, UK. Her latest poetry book, *The Waiting*, was published by Sahitya Akademi, India in 2019. She is the founder of Matwaala, the first South Asian Diaspora Poets Festival in the U.S.

Joel Allegretti, an American poet, is the author of *Platypus* (2017), a collection of poems, prose and performance texts, and *Our Dolphin* (2016), a novella. His second book of poems, *Father Silicon* (2006), was selected by *The Kansas City Star* as one of 100 Noteworthy Books of 2006. He is the editor of *Rabbit Ears: TV Poems* (2015). He wrote the texts for three song cycles by Frank Ezra Levy, whose work is released on Naxos American Classics. Allegretti is a member of the Academy of American Poets and ASCAP.

Sarah Allen, an American writer, is the author of *What Stars Are Made Of* and the upcoming *Breathing Underwater*. She is also

324 About the poets of Greening the Earth

a poet, and her work was published in *Presence*, *The Evansville Review*, *Quarter After Eight*, *Cicada*, *Birmingham Arts Journal* and more.

Michael Anania is an American poet, novelist and essayist. His modernist poetry meticulously evokes Midwestern prairies and rivers. His autobiographical novel, *Red Menace* (1984), captured mid-twentieth century cold war angst and the colloquial speech of Nebraska. His collections of poetry include *The Color of Dust* (1970), *Riversongs* (1978), *The Sky at Ashland* (1986), *Selected Poems* (1995), *Natural Light* (1999), *Heat Lines* (2005) and *Continuous Showings* (2017). He is a five-time winner of Illinois Arts Council Literary Awards (1974–1989) and the National Magazine Award (1981).

Issath Rehana Mohammed Azeem (Anar) is a distinguished voice in the Sri Lankan Tamil poetry scene with five critically acclaimed collections to her name. Her poems often address what it is like to be a Muslim woman living under war and violence. Her books have won several awards, most notably the Government of Sri Lanka's National Literature Award, the Tamil Literary Garden's (Canada) Poetry Award, Aaathmanam Award (Chennai), SPARROW Award (Mumbai) and the Vijay TV Excellence in the Field of Literature (Sigaram Thotta Pengal) Award.

Makhdoom Ammar Aziz is a poet and filmmaker from Pakistan. His multi-award-winning films have been screened in over a 100 countries at major film and art festivals. His poems often use personal narratives and fictional interventions in memories to examine spaces, bodies, objects and mythologies. He lives in Lahore.

Subhro Bandopadhyay is the author of four books of poetry in Bengali, one of which fetched him the Sahitya Akademi Yuva Puraskar in 2013. He received the Antonio Machado International Poetry Fellowship from the Government of Spain (2008) and Poetas de otros mundos distinction from Fondo Poético Internacional, Spain.

Jennifer Barber's books of poetry include *Works on Paper* (2016, winner of the 2015 Tenth Gate Prize), *Given Away* (2012) and *Rigging the Wind* (Kore Press, 2003, First Book Award). In 1992, she founded the literary journal *Salamander* based at Suffolk University, and served as its editor-in-chief through 2018. She lives in the Boston area, USA.

Ricardo Bellveser is a Spanish poet and a university professor. Among other awards, he has received the National Prize for Poetry Cultura Viva, the Prize of the Community of Castilla y León, the International Prize for Poetry Jaime Gil de Biedma, the University of León Prize for poetry, the Vicente Gaos Prize, the National Prize for the Promotion of Reading, the Prize for Valencian Literary Criticism and the Collective High Distinction of the Generalitat. He is the author of a dozen books of poetry that have been translated into Russian, French, Portuguese, Catalan, Serbian and English, about fifteen essays and anthologies and three novels. He is an elected correspondent academician of the Royal Academy of Fine Arts of San Carlos and an elected academician of the Valencian Academy of the Language.

Oscar René Benítez is originally a poet from El Salvador. He is now a naturalized American citizen and lives in California. The mayor of Los Angeles city, Tom Bradley, gave the City's Medal of Honor to Benítez for his cultural contribution to the Spanish speaking community. He is the vice president of Poetas del Mundo for the American Continent. He is very active and takes part in poetry readings around the world. Benítez has published eleven books.

Joanie Puma Bennet, an American poet, was fortunate to have inhabited a sheltered corner of the New York publishing world of the 1970s and 1980s—a niche at *The New Yorker*—and fortunate to have realized that even though it was fabulous, she was niche averse. This notion was reinforced at the Virginia Center for the Creative Arts and Blue Mountain Center in the Adirondacks. She's hiked and skied; her plays have been produced; she taught for the first time (for the University of Virginia's Young Writers Workshop) and travelled the country teaching and giving readings, including on the Navajo and Rosebud Sioux Reservations; and she recently moved to Santa Fe, New Mexico.

Richard Beregarten is an English and international poet. His writings have been translated into more than 100 languages and he has received numerous international awards. His chant-poem *TREE*, written in 1979 and first published in 1980, has appeared in many international contexts, including translations into more than a dozen languages. *TREE* is known as a key text in the worldwide ecological poetic movement. Berengarten lives in Cambridge, UK, where he teaches at Downing College and Pembroke College.

Tara Bergin was born and grew up in Dublin, Ireland. She is the author of two collections of poetry, *This is Yarrow* (2013, winner of the Seamus Heaney Prize for Poetry) and *The Tragic Death of Eleanor Marx* (2017, shortlisted for the T.S. Eliot and Forward Prizes).

Charles Bernstein is an American poet, essayist, editor and literary scholar. Bernstein is the Donald T. Regan professor emeritus at Department of English, University of Pennsylvania. In 2006, he was elected a fellow of the American Academy of Arts and Sciences and in 2019, he was awarded the Bollingen Prize from Yale University, the premier American prize for lifetime achievement that was conferred during the publication of *Near/ Miss* (2019). A volume of Bernstein's selected poetry from the past thirty years, *All the Whiskey in Heaven*, was published in 2010. *The Salt Companion to Charles Bernstein* was published in 2012.

Maren Bodenstein is a South African writer of German descent. She has published a novel, children's stories, short stories, flash fiction and essays. She is now working on a memoir trying to untangle her female ancestors from the nineteenth century German Lutheran missionary culture, which they were born into.

Coral Bracho was born in Mexico City. Her most recent poetry books include *Debe ser un malentendido* (2014) and *Poesía reunida 1977–2018* (2014). She has been a John Simon Guggenheim Fellow for poetry, and a Sistema Nacional de Creadores Fellow (México). She received the Xavier Villaurrutia Award in 2004 for *Ese espacio, ese jardín* (2004), the National Poetry Award (1981) for *El ser que va a morir* (1982) and the Latino World Poetry award, 2016.

Erin Holtz Braeckman is a Canadian poet. As an observer of the sacred in the everyday, a writer and an educator, she seeks to make 'the embodied inner life' a daily spiritual practice. She is a part-time faculty member at Lakefield College School, a reiki practitioner and an E-RYT with Yoga Alliance, teaching Hatha and Qigong out of her home business, The Village Yoga Studio in

Ontario, Canada. Erin is also the author of three published books and leads online programmes that explore rewilding the Earth-based ancestral wisdom traditions of the Deep Feminine.

Rafaella Del Bourgo's has won many awards including the Lullwater Prize for Poetry in 2003 and in 2006, the Helen Pappas Prize in Poetry and the New River Poets Award. The League of Minnesota Poets awarded her first place in 2009. In 2010, she won the Alan Ginsberg Poetry Award and the Grandmother Earth Poetry Prize. Her collection, *I Am Not Kissing You*, was published in 2003, and her chapbook, *Inexplicable Business: Poems Domestic and Wild*, was published in 2014. She has travelled the world and lived in Tasmania and Hawaii. She resides in Berkeley, California with her husband and one very spoiled cat.

Ann Bracken is the author of two collections of poetry, *No Barking in the Hallways: Poems from the Classroom (2017)* and *The Altar of Innocence* (2015). She serves as a contributing editor for *Little Patuxent Review*. Ann's poetry has garnered two nominations for the Pushcart Prize, and she co-facilitates Wilde Readings Poetry Series in Columbia, Maryland, USA.

Peter Brown's collection of short stories, *A Bright Soothing Noise* (2010), won the Katherine Anne Porter Prize. His translation of *Elsewhere on Earth* (2014) by the French poet Emmanuel Merle was longlisted for the National Translation Award in Poetry (ALTA). With co-translators, he edited and published a French translation of the collected poems of David Ferry.

Tsead Bruinja, who was the poet laureate of the Netherlands in 2019 and 2020, is a poet who actively searches for unknown, unfamiliar artistic grounds. In addition to being a poet, he is a critic, performer, editor, interviewer, teacher and, when a Frisian Bob Dylan tribute album was released, even a musician and singer.

Blake Campbell, a Pushcart Prize nominee, is the recipient of the 2015 Aliki Perroti and Seth Frank Most Promising Young Poet Award from the Academy of American Poets and a 2020 Emerging Artist Award from the St. Botolph Club Foundation.

Susana H. Case, an American poet, is the author of seven books of poetry, most recently *Dead Shark on the N Train* (2020), which won the Pinnacle Book Award for Best Poetry Book and NYC Big Book Award Distinguished Favorite. She is also the author of five chapbooks. Her first collection, *The Scottish Café* (2002), was re-released in a dual-language English-Polish version, *Kawiarnia Szkocka* (2010) and she has also been translated into Spanish, Italian and Portuguese. Case is a professor and program coordinator at the New York Institute of Technology in New York City.

Kenneth Carroll is a native Washingtonian and the former director of DC Writers Corps and the African American Writers Guild. He has taught at Duke Ellington School for the Arts, Washington Writers Center and Montgomery County Community College. He is a former Pushcart Prize nominee for poetry. He was featured in the Smithsonian Museum of African American Culture exhibit 'All the Stories Are True'.

Grace Cavalieri is an American poet, playwright and radio host of *The Poet and the Poem* from the Library of Congress. Poet Laureate of Maryland, Cavalieri has published many volumes of poetry and written twenty-six plays and two operas.

Priya Sarukkai Chabria is an award-winning poet, translator and writer who is acclaimed for her radical aesthetics across her ten books of poetry, speculative fiction, literary non-fiction, novel, and as editor of two poetry anthologies. *Andal The Autobiography of a Goddess,* translated from classical Tamil, won the Muse Translation Award 2017. *Slo-Glo* won the Experimental Fiction Award in The Best Asian Speculative Fiction Kitab Anthology. Priya edits *Poetry at Sangam.*

Sampurna Chattarji is an Indian Poet. She has published eighteen books, including a collection of short stories about Bombay/Mumbai, *Dirty Love* (2013), and seven poetry titles— the most recent being *Space Gulliver: Chronicles of an Alien* (2015). Her translations of Sukumar Ray and Joy Goswami have been published by Penguin and HarperCollins, respectively. She is poetry editor of *The Indian Quarterly.*

Maxine Chernoff is an American poet with an innovative, postmodern approach to her often surreal prose poetry. Her collections of poetry include A *Vegetable Emergency* (1977), *Utopia TV Store: prose poems* (1979), *New Faces of 1952* (1985), winner of the Carl Sandburg Award, *Leap Year Day: New and Selected Poems* (1990), *World: Poems 1991–2001,* and *Here* (2014). She is an editor of the journal *New American Writing* and a professor at San Francisco State University.

Robert Coats is an American poet and research hydrologist with the UC Davis Tahoe Environmental Research Center in the U.S. His book, *The Harsh Green World,* was published in 2015.

Geraldine Connolly is the author of a chapbook and four poetry collections including the recently published *Aileron* (2018). She has taught at the Writers Center in Bethesda in Maryland, The Chautauqua Institution and the University of Arizona Poetry Center. She has received fellowships from the National Endowment for the Arts, the Maryland Arts Council, and Breadloaf Writers Conference. She lives in Tucson, Arizona.

Michael Cope lives in Cape Town, South Africa. Michael has published a memoir, three collections of poetry, three novels and several chapbooks. He is a jeweller by profession.

Alfred Corn has published ten books of poems, including *Stake: Selected Poems, 1972-1992* (1999) and, most recently, *Unions* (2014). He has also published two novels, *Part of His Story* (1997) and *Miranda's Book* (2014), a study of prosody *The Poem's Heartbeat* (1997), and three collections of critical essays, *The Metamorphoses of Metaphor* (1987), *Atlas: Selected Essays, 1989-2007* (2008), and *Arks and Covenants: Essays and Aphorisms* (2017). Corn lives in Rhode Island and spends a part of every year in the UK.

Henry Crawford is an American poet. He is the author of two collections of poetry, *American Software* (2017) and the *Binary Planet* (2020). Henry is the host of the online reading series Poets vs The Pandemic.

Mamang Dai is a poet and novelist from Arunachal Pradesh, India. A former journalist and president of Arunachal Pradesh Union of Working Journalists, Dai's first publication *Arunachal Pradesh: The Hidden Land* (2003) received the state Verrier Elwin award. She has also worked with World Wide Fund for nature in the Eastern Himalaya Biodiversity Hotspots programme, and was member of the Arunachal Pradesh Public Service Commission (2011-2017). In 2011, Dai was awarded the Padma Shri. She received the Sahitya Akademi Award, 2017, for her book *The Black Hill* (2014) in English.

Mustansir Dalvi is an anglophone poet, translator and editor. His books of poems in English are *Brouhahas of Cocks* (2013), *Cosmopolitician* (2018) and *Walk* (2020). His 2012 English translation of Muhammad Iqbal's *Shikwa* and *Jawaab-e-Shikwa* as *Taking Issue and Allah's Answer* (Penguin Classics) has been described as 'insolent and heretical'. He is the editor of *Man without a Navel*, a collection of translations of Hemant Divate's poems from the Marathi. Mustansir Dalvi teaches architecture in Mumbai, India.

Keki Daruwalla is a major Indian poet writing in English. Author of over twelve books, he received the Sahitya Akademi award for his collection, *Keeper of the Dead* (1982). His *Collected Poems 1970–2005* was published by Penguin in 2006. He has also won the Commonwealth Poetry Award. He has also written novels such as *For Pepper and Christ* (2009) and *Ancestral Affairs* (2015).

Todd Davis is the author of six collections of poetry, most recently *Native Species* (2019) and *Winterkill* (2016). His writing has won the Foreword INDIES Book of the Year Bronze and Silver Awards, the Midwest Book Award, the Gwendolyn Brooks Poetry Prize, the Chautauqua Editors Prize, and the Bloomsburg University Book Prize. He teaches Environmental Studies at Pennsylvania State University's Altoona College, USA.

Ranajit Das is a Bengali poet from India with eleven collections of poetry, one novel and two collections of essays to his credit. He has also edited a collection of poetry from Bangladesh.

Lucille Lang Day, an American poet, is the author of seven full-length poetry collections and four chapbooks. Her latest collection is *Birds of San Pancho and Other Poems of Place* (November 2020). She has also co-edited two anthologies, *Fire and Rain: Ecopoetry of California* (2018) and *Red Indian Road West: Native American Poetry from California* (2018). She has also written a memoir, *Married at Fourteen: A True Story* (2012). Her many honours include the Blue Light Poetry Prize, two PEN Oakland/Josephine Miles Literary Awards, the Joseph Henry Jackson Award, and ten Pushcart Prize nominations. The founder and publisher of Scarlet Tanager Books. She lives in Oakland, California, with her husband, writer Richard Michael Levine.

Barry Dempster, a Canadian poet, has been twice nominated for the GG Award. He is the author of sixteen poetry collections, two novels and three previous books of stories. His poetry collection *The Burning Alphabet* won the Canadian Author's Association Award for Poetry. In 2014, he was shortlisted for the Trillium Award for his novel, *The Outside World*.

Toi Derricotte received the Frost Medal from Poetry Society of America in 2020. Her sixth collections of poetry, *I: New and Selected Poems*, was published in 2019 and shortlisted for the 2019 National Book Award. Her literary memoir, *The Black Notebooks* (1999) won the Anisfield-Wolf Book Award for Non-Fiction. With American writer and poet Cornelius Eady, Derricotte co-founded the Cave Canem Foundation. She is professor emerita from University of Pittsburgh and a former chancellor of the Academy of American Poets.

Hemang Desai is a bilingual Indian poet and translator working in Gujarati and English. His book-length English translations include

Poetic Refractions (2012), an anthology of contemporary Gujarati poetry, and *Thirsty Fish and other Stories* (2013), an anthology of select stories by eminent Gujarati writer 'Sundaram'. His Gujarati translations of Arun Kolatkar's *Kala Ghoda Poems (2004)* and *Sarpa Satra (2004)* have been published to critical acclaim.

Imtiaz Dharker is a British poet, artist and video filmmaker. Awarded the Queen's Gold Medal for Poetry, 2014, her six collections include *Over the Moon* (Bloodaxe Books, 2014) and *Luck Is the Hook* (Bloodaxe Books, 2018). Her poems have been featured widely on radio and television, as well as the London Underground and Mumbai buses.

Hemant Divate is a Marathi poet, editor, publisher and translator. He published *Struggles with Imagined Gods and Other Poems* (new translations) in 2019. He has a book each in Spanish, Irish, Arabic, German and Estonian apart from four in English. He has changed the Marathi literary scene through his little magazine *Abhidha Nantar* and Indian English poetry scene through Poetrywala.

Sharon Dolin is the author of six poetry collections: *Manual for Living* (2016), *Serious Pink* (2015), *Whirlwind* (2012), *Burn and Dodge* (2008, winner of the 2007 AWP Donald Hall Prize for Poetry), *Realm of the Possible* (2004), and *Heart Work* (1995). Her translation from Catalan of Gemma Gorga's *Book of Minutes* appeared in the Field Translation Series (2019) and her prose memoir, *Hitchcock Blonde* (2020). Among her awards are a 2016 PEN/Heim Translation Fund grant for her translations from Catalan, a 2013 Witter Bynner Fellowship from the Library of Congress, and a Pushcart Prize. She lives in New York City, where she is associate editor of Barrow Street Press and directs Writing About Art in Barcelona.

Ian Duhig is a British poet. He has written seven books of poetry, including the *The Blind Roadmaker* (2016), shortlisted for the Forward and T.S. Eliot Prizes. A Cholmondeley Award recipient, Duhig has won the Forward Best Poem Prize once and the National Poetry Competition twice. His *Selected Poems* are due from Picador in 2023.

Meg Eden, an American poet, is a 2020 Pitch Wars mentee. She teaches creative writing at Anne Arundel Community College in Maryland. She is the author of five poetry chapbooks, the novel *Post-High School Reality Quest* (2017), and the poetry collection *Drowning in the Floating World* (2020).

David Ebenbach is the author of seven books of poetry, fiction and non-fiction. He is also the winner of the Juniper Prize and the Drue Heinz Literature Prize. He lives with his family in Washington, D.C., where he teaches creative writing and literature at Georgetown University.

Mohsen Emadi is an Iranian/Mexican poet, translator, programmer and filmmaker. He is the author of seven books of poetry published in Spain, Iran, Mexico and the U.S. Emadi is the founder and editor of the *Persian Anthology of World Poetry*. As an active member of the Iranian Student Movement and then the Green Movement, he lived in exile in Finland, the Czech Republic, Spain and now, in Mexico. His poetic work has received various international awards.

Gail Rudd Entrekin, an American poet, is poetry editor of Hip Pocket Press and Editor of the online environmental literary magazine, *Canary*. She is editor of the poetry anthology *Yuba Flows* and the poetry and short fiction anthology *Sierra Songs & Descants:*

Poetry & Prose of the Sierra. Her five books of poetry include *The Art of Healing* with Charles Entrekin (2016), *Rearrangement of the Invisible* (2012) and *Change (Will Do You Good,* 2005), which was nominated for a Northern California Book Award.

Annie Finch is an American poet, critic, editor, translator, playwright and performer. Finch's first poetry collection, Eve (1997), was a finalist for the National Poetry Series and the Yale Series of Younger Poets. Calendars (2003), which was finalist for the National Poetry Series and shortlisted for the Forward Poetry Book of the Year award, is structured around a series of poems written for performance to celebrate the Wheel of the Year. Her third book, Among the Goddesses: An Epic Libretto in Seven Dreams (2010) received the Sarasvati Award for Poetry.

Maria Galina, a poet, writer, critic and translator, writes both literary and science fiction. She is the author of the novels *Volchja Zviezda* (also known as *The Wolf Star,* AST, *2004*), *Iramification* (English version of *Givi and Shenderovich,* Mosty kul'tury, 2004). *Iramification* won the award for the best science-fiction/fantasy novel of International Assembly Portal, Kiev, Ukraine in 2005 and Academia Rossica award for the best translation from Russian, Great Britain, 2009. Her work, *Malaya Glusha* (2009) was shortlisted for the the Big Book (Bolshaya Kniga) award 2009, and longlisted for the Russian Booker Award. Galina's *Ground Crayfish* (2011) was selected as reader's choice for the Big Book award, 2012. Her *Autochthons* (2015) was shortlisted and selected as reader's choice for the Big Book award and shortlisted for the National Bestseller award. Galina currently works for Russia's oldest literary magazine *Novy Mir* (Moscow) as the deputy governor of the Department of Literature Critique and Social Problems and as a columnist.

Kevin Gallagher is a poet, publisher and political economist living in Boston. His recent books are *And Yet it Moves* (2021), *Radio Plays* (2019), and *Loom* (2021). He edits *spoKe*, a Boston area annual of poetry and poetics.

Forrest Gander is the author of several collections of poetry, including *Be With* (2018), winner of the 2019 Pulitzer Prize in Poetry. The collection was also longlisted for the 2018 National Book Award in Poetry. His collection *Core Samples from the World* (2011) was a finalist for the 2012 Pulitzer Prize.

Antonio Gamoneda is a Spanish poet, winner of the Cervantes Prize in 2006. He has also been awarded the Gold Medal of the city of Pau, the Silver Medal of Asturias, the 'Lete' Gold Medal of the Province of León and the Gold Medal of the Círculo de Bellas Artes. He is Doctor Honoris Causa by the University of León.

Dawn Garisch is a poet from South Africa with two collections, including *Disturbance*, published in 2020.

Rainer Maria Gassen is a bilingual German poet who has published more than ten volumes of poetry. He has taught German and English in England and in Germany.

Christine Gelineau is the author of the poetry collections *Crave* (2016) and *Remorseless Loyalty* (winner of the Snyder Prize); as well as the book-length sequence *Appetite for the Divine* (Editor's Choice for the McGovern Prize from Ashland). A recipient of the Pushcart Prize, Gelineau teaches in the Maslow Family Graduate Program in Creative Writing at Wilkes University, U.S.

P.N. Gopikrishnan has five books of poems and four works of translation in different genres. He has also authored four film scripts. He has won six awards, including the Kerala Sahitya Akademi award. Gopikrishnan is a senior manager of Kerala State Financial Enterprises.

J.P. Grasser, an American poet, is a former Wallace Stegner fellow at Stanford University. He is the recipient of the inaugural Tree Climate Action Poem Prize from Academy of American Poets as well as the 2019 Open Prize from *Frontier Poetry.*

Hywel Griffiths is an academic working in the Department of Geography and Earth Sciences at the Aberystwyth University in Wales. He is a highly recognized Welsh poet.

Adalet Barış Günersel was born in Istanbul, Turkey. She now lives in the U.S. Her book, *A Year in Rio,* was published in Turkish (2005).

Kimiko Hahn is the author of ten collections of poetry, most recently, *Foreign Bodies* (2020). Her subject matter often concerns our planet. She is a distinguished professor at Queens College, the City University of New York where she teaches in the MFA Program.

Anna Halberstadt is a poet and a translator. She has published four collections of poetry, *Vilnius Diary* (2014), *Transit* (2016), *Green in a Landscape with Ashes* and *Gloomy Sun* (2018), and two books of translations of American poetry, *Selected Selected* by Eileen Myles (2017) and *Nocturnal Fire* by Edward Hirsch (2017), into Russian. She is a recipient of several awards, such as the International Merit Award by *Atlanta Review*, two nominations for Pushcart award by the *Mudfish* journal and others.

Richard Harteis is an American poet and novelist. He is the president of the William Meredith Foundation and directs Poets Choice Publishing House. He has written fourteen books of prose and poetry and edited and introduced twelve books with publishers in Bulgaria and abroad.

John Hennessy's collections include *Coney Island Pilgrims* (2013) and *Bridge and Tunnel* (2007). He teaches at the University of Massachusetts and serves as poetry editor for *The Common*.

W.N. Herbert, a Scottish poet from Dundee, Scotland, is also a professor of poetry and creative Writing at Newcastle University. He was one of the writers involved in the informationist poetry movement that emerged in Scotland in the 1990s. He is also considered a New Generation poet.

Scott Hightower has authored poetry books such as *Tin Can Tourist* (2001), *Natural Trouble* (2001), *Part of the Bargain* (2005); it received the Hayden Carruth Award), *Self-Evident* (2012), and *Hontanares* (also previously in the Devenir el otro series, 2012). Hightower is the editor of the bilingual anthology, *Women Rowing: Mujeres A Los Remos*. His translations of Spanish poetry have won a Willis Barnstone Translation Prize. He is a native of central Texas.

Geoffrey Himes is an American poet and lyricist. His song lyrics have been set to music by Si Kahn, Walter Egan, Pete Kennedy, Billy Kemp, Fred Koller and others. His book on Bruce Springsteen, *Born in the USA*, was published in 2005. He has written about popular music and theatre for the *Washington Post, New York Times, Rolling Stone, Smithsonian Magazine, Paste, Downbeat, Sing Out* and the *Nashville Scene* since 1977.

Paul Hoover is an American poet whose writings have been associated with the New York School and language poetry. He is a professor of creative writing at San Francisco State University in California. He is also the editor, with Maxine Chernoff, of the literary magazine, *New American Writing*. He is also known for editing the anthology, *Postmodern American Poetry*, first published in 1994.

Robert A. Hueckstedt translates from Hindi and Sanskrit. His translation from the Hindi include a novel by Manohar Shyam Joshi, *The Perplexity of Hariya Hercules* (2009). He teaches at the University of Virginia.

Major Jackson is an American poet and professor. He is the author of five collections of poetry, *The Absurd Man* (2020), *Roll Deep* (2015), *Holding Company* (2010) and *Hoops* (2006). *Hoops* was selected as a finalist for an NAACP Image Award for Outstanding Literature-Poetry, and *Leaving Saturn* (2002) won the 2000 Cave Canem Poetry Prize and was a finalist for a National Book Critics Award Circle.

W. Luther Jett is a retired special educator from Montgomery County, Maryland, U.S. He is the author of the poetry chapbooks, *Not Quite: Poems Written in Search of My Father*, released in the fall of 2015, and *Our Situation* released in summer 2018. A third chapbook, *Everyone Disappears*, was published in 2020 and an additional chapbook, *Little Wars*, was published in 2021.

Dileep Jhaveri writes poetry in Gujarati and English. An anthologist, translator, memoirist and playwright, he is a physician practicing in Thane, Mumbai. His poems have been translated into many Indian and foreign languages and published.

Luz Elena Sepúlveda Jimenez was born in Medellin, Colombia. She has published *A Soul Made Landscape* (2013), *The Compass of Light* (2015), *Ecstatic of Worlds* (2016) and *Un tris de Café* (2018).

Krishna Mohan Jha, a poet and literary critique, writes both in Hindi and Maithili; has published two collections of poems, *Samay Ko Cheerkar* (1998) and *Ekta Herayal Duniya* (2008). Jha has edited *Bhanai Vidyapati* (2003), and assisted in editing of *Tana Bana* (2000). He has received Kanhaiya Smriti Samman (1998), Hemant Smriti Kavita Puraskar (2003) and Kirti Narayan Mishra Sahitya Samman (2013). He is currently a professor at the Department of Hindi in Assam University, Silchar, Assam.

Deryn Rees-Jones, a British poet and critic, is the editor of *Pavilion Poetry*. Recent books include *Paula Rego: The Art of Story* (2019) a study of the Portuguese artist, and *Fires*, a lyrical essay (2019). Her selected poems *What It's Like to Be Alive*, was published by Seren in 2016. *Erato,* her fifth collection, was shortlisted for the Welsh Book of the Year and the T.S. Eliot Prize. She is professor of poetry at the University of Liverpool.

S. Joseph is an important Malayalam Dalit poet with four collections of poetry, including *Identity Card* and *Meenkara*n. He is a Kerala Sahitya Akademi awardee and has a collection of prose writings. He has also taught at Maharaja's College, Kochi, Kerala.

Katia Kapovich, originally from Moldova, lives in Cambridge, MA. She is the author of ten Russian poetry collections and of two volumes of English verse, *Gogol in Rome* (Salt, 2004), which was shortlisted for England's 2005 Jerwood Alderburgh Prize, and *Cossacks and Bandits* (2008). In 2019, she received the (Russian) Hemingway Prize for a short story collection.

Vincent Katz is an American poet and translator, who lives in New York city. His most recent publication is a book of poems, *Broadway for Paul* (2020). He has published translations of the Roman poet Sextus Propertius (2004), which won the National Translation Award and is working on a translation of Hesiod's *Theogony* and *Works and Days* (2015). He is the author of the poetry collections *Swimming Home* (2015) and *Southness* (2016).

Sachin C. Ketkar is a bilingual writer, translator, editor, blogger and researcher based in Baroda, Gujarat, India. His collections of Marathi poetry include *Jarasandhachya Blogvarche Kahi Ansh* (2010) and *Bhintishivaicya Khidkitun Dokavtana* (2004). His books in English include *Skin, Spam and Other Fake Encounters: Selected Marathi Poems in translation* (2011), and *A Dirge for the Dead Dog and Other Incantations* (2003). He has extensively translated present-day Marathi poetry, most of which is collected in the anthology *Live Update: An Anthology of Recent Marathi Poetry,* (2005). He won the Indian Literature Poetry Translation Prize given by *Indian Literature Journal,* Sahitya Akademi, New Delhi for translation of modern Gujarati poetry in 2000. He works as professor of English, faculty of arts at The Maharaja Sayajirao University of Baroda, Vadodara. Currently, he is working on *A Critical History of Marathi Literature.*

Christopher (Kit) Kelen, a poet and painter, resides in the Myall Lakes of New South Wales, Australia. Published widely since the seventies, he has a dozen full length collections in English as well as translated books of poetry in Chinese, Portuguese, French, Italian, Spanish, Indonesian, Swedish, Norwegian and Filipino. His latest volume of poetry in English is *Poor Man's Coat—Hardanger Poems,* published in 2018. In 2017, Kit was shortlisted twice for the Montreal Poetry Prize and won the Local Award in the Newcastle Poetry Prize.

Sarah Key has written eight cookbooks, essays on the *Huffington Post*, and more poems than she can count. She published *Put into Words My Love* in 2020. She now learns from her students at a community college in the South Bronx in New York where she is poet in practice.

Mimi Khalvati is an Iranian-born British poet. She has published nine collections with Carcanet Press, including *The Meanest Flower* (2007), which was shortlisted for the T.S. Eliot Prize. *Child: New and Selected Poems 1991-2011* was a Poetry Book Society Special Commendation and her most recent, *Afterwardness*, is a PBS Winter Wild Card. She is a fellow of the Royal Society of Literature.

John Kinsella is an Australian poet and novelist. He has published over thirty books and he has won many awards for his poetry. Kinsella now teaches at Cambridge University.

Ashwani Kumar is an Indian poet, writer and professor at Tata Institute of Social Sciences, Mumbai. His work, *Architecture of Alphabets*, a volume of his select poems has been translated in Hungarian. He is also co-founder of Indian Novels Collective for translation of classic Indian language novels.

Nilim Kumar is an Indian poet who writes in Assamese. He has written twenty collection of poems, three novels and one book of essays. He is the recipient of Uday Bharati National Award, Raza Foundation award, Shabda award and Ramanath Bhattacharya Foundation award.

Sukrita Paul Kumar is an Indian poet and critic. She was an invited poet and fellow at the prestigious International Writing

Programme, Iowa, U.S. She is a former fellow of the Indian Institute of Advanced Study, Shimla, and honorary faculty at Durrell Centre at Corfu, Greece. She has published several collections of poetry, translations and critical works.

Susanna Lang, an American poet, lives and teaches in Chicago. Her chapbook, *Self-Portraits,* was released in October 2020, and her translation of *Baalbek* by Nohad Salameh was published by L'Atelier du Grand Tétras in 2021. Her third full-length collection of poems, *Travel Notes from the River Styx,* was published in 2017. Her translations of poetry by Yves Bonnefoy include *Words in Stone* and *The Origin of Language.* She is now working with Souad Labbize on new translations.

Hiram Larew is an American poet and entomologist. His *Poetry X Hunger* initiative is bringing poets from around the world for the anti-hunger cause. He lives in Maryland, U.S.

B.J. Lee is a former music librarian at the Boston Conservatory at Berklee turned full-time writer and poet. Her debut picture book, *There Was an Old Gator Who Swallowed a Moth*, was released in 2019. She is an award-winning poet with over 100 poems published/forthcoming in major anthologies by such publishers as Little, Brown, National Geographic, Bloomsbury, Eerdmans, Wordsong, Otter-Barry and others. She blogs at *Today's Little Ditty*, where she is an authority on poetic forms.

Tim Liardet has been twice shortlisted for the T.S. Eliot Prize, for *The World Before Snow* in 2015 and *The Blood Choir* in 2006. He has produced ten collections of poetry to date. He has also been longlisted for the Whitbread Poetry Prize, and has received several Poetry Book Society recommendations, a Poetry Book Society

Pamphlet Choice, an Arts Council England Writer's award, a Society of Authors award, a Hawthornden fellowship, three Pushcart nominations, and various other awards. In September 2019, he received an Authors' Foundation work-in-progress award from the Society of Authors. From 2015 to 2018, he was a Poetry Book Society selector and is currently professor of poetry at Bath Spa University, UK.

Maria Lisella, the sixth Queens Poet Laureate, was awarded a Poet Laureate fellowship by the Academy of American Poets. Her collections include *Thieves in the Family* (NYQ Books, 2014), and two chapbooks: *Amore on Hope Street* (Finishing Line Press, 2009) and *Two Naked Feet* (Poets Wear Prada, 2009). She is the New York culture correspondent for the *Jerusalem Post*.

Charlotte Mandel's eleventh book of poetry is titled *Alive and in Use: Poems in the Japanese Form of Haibun* (2019). Her chapbook, *Light's Music*, is included in Delphi Series 8 (2020). She has received a lifetime achievement award from Brooklyn College, New Jersey poets prize and two fellowships in poetry from the New Jersey State Council on the Arts. She has edited the Eileen W. Barnes award anthology of older women poets, *Saturday's Women*.

Herbert Woodward Martin, an American poet, has studied with Karl Shapiro, Frederick Will and Millier Williams among others. He is the author of ten volumes of poetry and has collaborated with American composers, Joseph Fennimore and Phillip Mahugsson. With composer Adolphus Hailstork, Martin has written the librettos for two Concert Arias, and the text for *Crispus Attucks and A Knee on the Neck: A Requiem*.

Stephen Massimilla is a poet, scholar, professor, and painter. His multi-genre volume, *Cooking with the Muse* (2016), won the Eric Hoffer Book award, the National Indie Excellence award, the Independent Author Network Book of the Year award, and many others. He is the editor of *Stronger than Fear* (2022). His previous books and awards include *The Plague Doctor in His Hull-Shaped Hat* (an SFASU Press Prize selection), *Forty Floors from Yesterday* (winner of the Bordighera/CUNY Poetry Prize), *Later on Aiaia* (Grolier Poetry Prize winner). Massimilla teaches at Columbia University and The New School.

Monica Mody is the author of Kala Pani and two cross-genre chapbooks. Her poetry has also appeared in literary journals and anthologies including Poetry International, Indian Quarterly, Boston Review, and Almost Island. Her awards include the Nicholas Sparks Postgraduate Writing Fellowship at the University of Notre Dame, Naropa University's Zora Neale Hurston Award, and the Toto Funds the Arts Award for Creative Writing. Mody has a PhD in East West Psychology from the California Institute of Integral Studies.

Sharmistha Mohanty is a fiction writer and poet living in Mumbai. Her most recent work is *Five Movements in Praise* (2013).

Sonnet Mondal is an Indian poet, literary curator, editor, and author of *An Afternoon in My Mind* (2022), *Karmic Chanting* (2018) and *Ink and Line* (2018).

Daniel Thomas Moran, former Poet Laureate of Suffolk County, New York, is the author of twelve volumes of poetry, the most recent of which, *In the Kingdom of Autumn*, was published in 2020 and *Balance*, also in 2020.

David Morley is an ecologist, poet, editor and teacher. Emerging with *Releasing Stone* (1989), he has since published five collections, the most recent, *The Invisible Gift: Selected Poems* (2015). It won the 2015 Ted Hughes Award. His previous collection, *The Gypsy and the Poet*, was a PBS Recommendation.

Tim J. Myers is a writer, songwriter, storyteller and senior lecturer at Santa Clara University, U.S. He's published over 130 poems, won a first prize in a poetry contest judged by John Updike, has four books of adult poetry, won a major prize in science fiction, and has been nominated for two Pushcart Prizes.

Philip Nikolayev is a Russo-American bilingual poet living in Boston. He is the author of several volumes of poetry and translations. Nikolayev is also a polyglot and translates poetry from several languages. Nikolayev's collections include *Monkey Time* (winner of the 2001 Verse Prize) and *Letters from Aldenderry* (2006). He co-edits *Fulcrum*, a serial anthology of poetry and critical writing.

Diane Wilbon Parks is an American poet, visual artist and author with two collections of poetry, including *The Wisdom of Blue Apples* (2016). She is an honouree of Prince George's County Poets of Excellence. One of her poems has been turned into a permanent installation at Patuxent Research Refuge in Maryland. She is the founder of The Write Blend poetry ensemble. She is a senior IT programme manager and a U.S. Airforce veteran and lives in Maryland.

Shara McCallum, originally from Jamaica, is the author of six books published in the U.S. and UK, including *No Ruined Stone* (2021), a verse sequence based on an alternate account of history and Scottish poet Robert Burns' near migration to Jamaica to work on a slave plantation. Her book, *Madwoman* (2017), received the 2018 OCM Bocas Prize for Caribbean Poetry and the 2018 Motton Book Prize from the New England Poetry Club. McCallum is a Liberal Arts professor of English at Penn State University and on the faculty of the Pacific University Low-Residency MFA Program.

Bruce McRae, a Canadian musician currently residing on Salt Spring Island in British Columbia, is a multiple Pushcart nominee. He has written books such as *The So-Called Sonnets* (2010), *An Unbecoming Fit of Frenzy* (2015), *Like as if* (2016) and *Hearsay.*

Arvind Krishna Mehrotra has published six collections of poetry in English and two of translation—a volume of Prakrit love poems, *The Absent Traveller* (2008), and *Songs of Kabir* (2011). His *Oxford India Anthology of Twelve Modern Indian Poets* (1997) has been very influential. He has edited several books, including *History of Indian Literature in English* (2003) and *Collected Poems in English* by Arun Kolatkar (2010). His collection of essays *Partial Recall: Essays on Literature and Literary History* was published in 2012 and *Translating the Indian Past* in 2019.

Vivek Narayanan's books of poems include *Universal Beach* (Harbour Line Press, 2006), *Life and Times of Mr S* (2020), and *AFTER: A Writing Through Valmiki's Ramayana* (2022). His translations include poems by Kutti Revathi, done in collaboration with Padma Narayanan and the author, that have appeared in *Asymptote*, *The Wire*, and *Modern Poetry in Translation*; and also an ongoing current project, the *Kuruntokai*, an ancient Tamil anthology of short poems.

Rimi Nath an assistant professor in the Department of English, North-Eastern Hill University. Her poems have appeared in several national journals.

Robin S. Ngangom is a bilingual poet from Manipur, India, who writes in English and Meiteilon. His books of poetry include *Words and the Silence (1988)*, *Time's Crossroads (1994)* and *The Desire of Roots (2006)*. He was conferred with the Katha Award for Translation in 1999   .

Stanley Niamatali, a Guyanan poet, is a professor of English at Montgomery College, in Rockville, Maryland. His poetry has been published by Oberon, Full Circle and Anthology of Appalachian Writers and The Caribbean Writer.

Kynpham Sing Nongkynrih writes poems, short fiction and drama in Khasi and English. He has a total of thirteen publications in Khasi. His collections of poetry in English include *Moments*, *The Sieve* and *The Yearning of Seeds*.

Jean Nordhaus earned an undergraduate degree in philosophy from Barnard College and a PhD in German literature from Yale University. She is the author of the poetry chapbook *A Language of Hands* (1982) as well as the collections *A Bracelet of Lies* (1987), *The Porcelain Apes of Moses Mendelssohn* (2002), *Innocence* (2006) and *Memos from the Broken World* (2016).

Fan Ogilvie is the second Poet Laureate of West Tisbury, and co-founder of Featherstone Festival of Poetry. Her published work includes, *YOU selected poems* and *KNOT: A Life*. Her new poetry collection is *Easinesses Found*.

Amir Or is an Israeli poet, novelist, and essayist whose works have been published in 45 languages. He is the author of twelve volumes of poetry. His most recent books in Hebrew are *The Madman's Prophecy, Loot and Wings*.

Sabine Pascarelli is an Italian poet from Tuscany who grew up in Germany. She is a published poet, an author of children's literature and a translator of English, German and Italian. Her works of translated poems include *The Alchemy of Grief* by Emily Ferrara (2007), winner of the Bardighero Poetry Award in 2007, *Repubblica* (2013) by Dr J.H. Beall and *Casa forei per amore* by Grace Cavalieri.

Keith Payne is an award-winning poet and translator. His debut collection of poems, *Broken Hill* (2015) was followed by several translations: *Six Galician Poets* (from the Galican, 2016), *Museums, Rooms and Trees*, (from the Spanish of Marta Fernández Calvo, 2017), *Diary of Crosses Green* (from the Galician of Martín Veiga, 2018), *Elevation of the Ruin* (from the Spanish of Aníbal Núñez, 2018) and *Second Tongue* (from the Galician of Yolanda Castaño, 2020). He is founder-director of the International Poetry Festival Poema Ria Vigo and The La Malinche Readings between Ireland and Galicia.

Sharmila Pokharel is an Edmonton-based poet, born and raised in Nepal. Her bilingual poetry collection, *My Country Foreign Land* was published in 2014 (Co-translator: Alice Major). She has received the 2012 Cultural Diversity in the Arts Award from the Edmonton Arts Council. She is a co-author of *Somnio; The Way We See It*, a poetry and art book project, published in 2015. This book has received the 2014 Cultural Diversity in the Arts Project grant. She has been working on her memoir, *A Village of Happy Faces*.

Rochelle Potkar is the author of *Four Degrees of Separation* and *Paper Asylum*—shortlisted for the Rabindranath Tagore Literary Prize 2020. Her poetry film *Skirt* was showcased on American showrunner Shonda Rhimes' Shondaland in 2018. Her poems *To Daraza* won the 2018 Norton Girault Literary Prize UK, and *The Girl from Lal Bazaar* was shortlisted for the Gregory O' Donoghue International Poetry Prize, 2018.

M.P. Pratheesh is an Indian poet and photographer. He has published six collections of poetry in Malayalam. His poems or images have appeared in *Kavyabharati, The Bombay Review, Keralakavitha, Guftugu.in* and *Indian Literature.*

Pratishtha Pandya is a bilingual poet and translator working across Gujarati and English.

Alvin Pang is a poet, writer, editor, anthologist and translator. He was Singapore's Young Artist of the Year for Literature in 2005 and received the Singapore Youth Award for Arts and Culture in 2007, and the JCCI Foundation Education Award in 2008. His poems have been translated into over fifteen languages, and he has appeared in major festivals and publications worldwide.

Linda Pastan was an American poet of Jewish background. From 1991 to 1995 she was Poet Laureate of Maryland. Pastan's many awards include the Dylan Thomas award, a Pushcart Prize, the Bess Hokin Prize from Poetry, the Poetry Society of America's Alice Fay di Castagnola Award, and the Ruth Lilly Poetry Prize, in 2003.

Erin Petti is a writer who specializes in stories for young people. She lives in New England. She is the author of The Peculiar Haunting of Thelma Bee.

Blas Muñoz Pizarro is one of the most outstanding and laureate poets of Spanish letters. He has won numerous awards since 1971 with a first stage of creation. In 2007, he wrote *La mirada de Jano*, which won the prestigious 2008 Paco Mollá Poetry Prize.

Q.R. Quasar (aka David Martin) is an American poet, playwright, novelist and scholar/translator of Arabic and Persian poetry and philosophy. His titles include, *Watching the Universe Die*, *The Universe in Bloom, Ocean of Suns*, and *Buddha Time*. Quasar lives in Montgomery County, Maryland.

Barbara Quick has published a chapbook, *The Light of Sifnos*, that won the 2020 Blue Light Press Poetry Prize and published in 2021.

Ann Quinn is a poet, editor, teacher, mentor, mother and classical clarinettist. Her chapbook, *Final Deployment*, has been published by Finishing Line Press in 2018. She teaches at the Writer's Center in Bethesda and is the poetry editor for *Yellow Arrow Journal*.

Anupama Raju is a poet, communications professional, literary journalist and translator. She is the author of *Nine*, and has been featured in several poetry anthologies. She collaborated with French photographer Pascal Bernard on two Indo-French poetry and photography projects 'Surfaces and Depths' (2012–2013) and 'Une Ville, Un Lieu, Une Personne' (2011–2012).

P. Raman has three collections of poetry including *Kanam*. He has also translated chosen poets from abroad. He edits a poetry magazine, *Thilanila* (Boiling Point) and has won the Kerala Sahitya Akademi award among others. His poems have been translated into Tamil and English.

P.P. Ramachandran has three collections of poetry, including the first collection *Kaanekkaane* (Watching) that won the Kerala Sahitya Akademi award. His interests lie in amateur theatre and web publishing. His poems have been translated into English and Tamil and he runs an online poetry magazine, *Harithakam.com*

Yaxkin Melchy Ramos, born in Mexico City, is a poet, artisan-editor and eco-poetics/biodiversity researcher. Over ten years, he wrote a 'seedbed' book of scientific and poetic language called *The New World*, several parts of which have been published. In 2009, he won the Elías Nandino National Youth Poetry Prize, and in 2010 the Navachiste Festival's Interamerican Poetry Prize. His publications include, *Hatun Mayu* (2016), about his experience with traditional indigenous medicine and *Pedregal Meditations* (2019) about the volcanic ecosystem of Pedregal de San Ángel. He lives and studies in Japan and has translated poems of Nanao Sakaki into Spanish.

Santiago Rodríguez is a senior lecturer at the University of Valladolid (Spain), where he teaches American Literature. He has edited an anthology of American short fiction, *Pioneros: Cuentos norteamericanos del siglo XIX* (2011). He has also translated and edited Henry James' *Daisy Miller, The Turn of the Screw, The Beast in the Jungle* and *The Jolly Corner* (2005) and Walt Whitman's *Specimen Days* (2019).

Bobby C. Rogers is the author of *Paper Anniversary* (2010), which won the Agnes Lynch Starrett Prize, and *Social History* (2016). He lives in Memphis, Tennessee, U.S.

Jamie B. Rosa was born in Bellreguard-Valencia in Spain. He studied philosophy at University of Valencia. He has published thirteen books of poetry, seven novels and several anthologies about cultures of the world.

Gabriel Rosenstock is an Irish poet, playwright, haikuist, tankaist, essayist and author/translator of over 180 books, mostly in Irish. He has edited and contributed to books of haiku in Irish, English, Scottish and Japanese. He has translated several international poets such as Ko Un, Seamus Heaney, K. Satchidanandan, Rabindranath Tagore and Muhammad Iqbal into Irish. He has also translated plays of Samuel Beckett, Max Frisch and William Butler Yeats and songs by Bob Dylan, Leonard Cohen and Bob Marley. He has twenty poetry collections in Irish and eleven in English, besides several essays to his name.

Michael Rothenberg is an American poet, songwriter, editor, artist, and environmentalist. In 2016, Rothenberg moved to Tallahassee, Florida where he has been working as the Florida State University Libraries Poet in Residence. In 1989, Rothenberg and artist Nancy Davis began Big Bridge Press, a fine print literary press. It has published works of poets such as Jim Harrison, Joanne Kyger, Allen Ginsberg, Philip Whalen, Michael McClure and others. Rothenberg is editor of *Big Bridge*, a webzine of poetry. He is also co-editor and co-founder of *Jack* Magazine.

Cheran Rudramoorthy is a Tamil Indian poet living and working in Canada. He has published eleven anthologies of poetry in Tamil. His poems have been translated into twenty-one languages including Spanish, Kannada, Malayalam, Dutch, Bangla and Telugu. He is a professor of sociology at the university of Windsor, Canada.

Abdul Hadi Sadoun is a writer, researcher and hispanist from Baghdad, Iraq, who lives in Madrid. He has written books in

Arabic and Spanish. His notable Spanish publications include, *Cuneiform* (2006), *Familiar Plagiarism* (2008), *Bird in the Mouth and Other Poems* (2009), *Always, Always* (2010), *Fields of the Stranger* (2011) and *Memories of an Iraqi Dog* (2016). His work, *They Are Not Verses What I Write*, a short anthology of Darmi, the Iraq's *Women Popular Songs*, was published in 2018.

Margaret R. Sáraco is an American writer, performer, educator and activist. Her poetry has appeared in anthologies and journals including *Show us Your Papers, Peregrine Journal, Lips, Exit 13, Poeming Pigeon* and the *Paterson Literary Review*. She won Honorable Mention in the 2020.

Omar Sakr, born in Western Sydney, is the son of Lebanese and Turkish Muslim migrants. He is the author of two collections of poetry, *These Wild Houses* (2017) and *The Lost Arabs* (2020), which was shortlisted for the 2020 NSW Premier's Literary Awards, the 2020 Queensland Literary Awards, the 2020 John Bray Poetry Award, the 2020 Colin Roderick Award, and the 2020 Prime Minister's Literary Award for Poetry. In 2019, he received the Edward Stanley Award for Poetry, and in 2020 the Woollahra Digital Literary Prize for Poetry.

Igor Satanovsky, born in in Kiev, is a bilingual Russian-American poet, editor, translator, curator and visual artist who arrived in the U.S. as a Soviet refugee in 1989. His latest publication is Swype Revelations, a bilingual chapbook of poetic collaborations with *AI* (2021). Currently, he is senior book designer at Sterling Publishing and chief editor of Novaya Kozha, a Russian-language almanac of arts and letters.

Jane Satterfield's recent work includes *Apocalypse Mix* (2017). Satterfield has been awarded Autumn House Poetry Prize, 49th

Parallel Prize from Bellingham Review, Ledbury poetry prize and National Endowment for the Arts Poetry fellowship. Jane is a professor of writing in Loyola University, Maryland and lives in Baltimore.

Jane Schapiro is an American poet and author of three volumes of poetry: *Tapping This Stone* (1995), *Let The Wind Push Us Across* (2017), and *Warbler* (2020). She is also the author of the nonfiction book *Inside a Class Action: The Holocaust and the Swiss Banks* (2003) selected for the Notable Trials Library. Her chapbook *Mrs Cave's House* won the 2012 Sow's Ear Poetry Chapbook competition.

Shafi Shauq is a Kashmiri poet, fiction writer, professor, and lexicographer. He is the author/editor/translator of over seventy-five books in Kashmiri, English, Urdu and Hindi. Shauq has received the Sahitya Akademi Award in creative writing (2006), Bharti Bhasha Samman Award (2007), Sahitya Akademi Translation Award (2007), Ahad Zargar award (2011) and State Award for Outstanding Contribution (2014). Shauq has been associated with several national academic projects like *Encyclopaedia of Indian Literature*, *Medieval Indian Literature*, and *Oxford Companion to Indian Theatre*. Some of his best known books are: *Yaad Aasmaanan Hinz* (Remembering the Skies, poetry), *Zabaan ti Adab* (language and literature; Criticism), *Kaeshur Lughaat* (Kashmiri Dictionary), *Aa Kini* (yes or no, poetry) and *Kaeshir Zabaan ti Adabuk Tavaearyiekh* (history of the Kashmiri language and literature).

Clare Shaw lives in West Yorkshire in the North of England. She has written poetry collections such as *Straight Ahead* (2006), *Head on* (2012), *Flood* (2018) and *Towards a General Theory of Love* (2022).

H.S. Shivaprakash is an Indian poet, playwright, critic, translator and columnist writing in Kannada. He has published thirteen poetry books in Kannada and four in English, fourteen plays and seven prose works in Kannada and English. He was a former editor of *Indian Literature* and former director of the Tagore Centre, Berlin.

Sean Singer is the author of *Discography* (2002), winner of the Yale Series of Younger Poets Prize, and the Norma Farber First Book Award from the Poetry Society of America and a fellowship from the National Endowment for the Arts. His other works include *Honey & Smoke* (2015) and *Today in the Taxi* (2022).

Larissa Shmailo is a poet, novelist, translator, editor and critic. She has written novels like *Sly Bang* (2018) and *Patient Women* (2015). Her poetry collections are *Medusa's Country* (2017), *#specialcharacters* (2014), *In Paran*, the chapbook *A Cure for Suicide* (2008), and the e-book *Fib Sequence* (2011). Shmailo's work has appeared in the anthologies *Measure for Measure: An Anthology of Poetic Meters* (2015), *Contemporary Russian Poetry* (2008) and *Choice Words: Writers on Abortion* (2020).

Laura Shovan is a Pushcart Prize-nominated poet, editor and author of children's books.

Penelope Shuttle's thirteenth collection, *Lyonesse*, was published by Bloodaxe Books in 2021; *Encounters on a Bench*, her radio poem, was broadcast on BBC Radio 4 in 2020; a pamphlet, *Father Lear*, was published by *Poetry Salzburg* in 2020 and *Will You Walk a Little Faster?* was published in 2017.

Ndaba Sibanda, an African poet, has received the Pushcart Prize and Best of the Net nominations. Some of his work has been translated into Serbian. His works include *Notes, Themes, Things And Other Things, The Gushungo Way, Sleeping Rivers, Love O'clock, The Dead Must Be Sobbing, Football of Fools, Cutting-edge Cache, Of the Saliva and the Tongue, When Inspiration Sings In Silence, The Way Forward* and more. He hails from Zimbabwe, but currently lives in Ethiopia.

Malachi Smith is a fellow of the University of Miami's Mitchner Caribbean Writer's Institute, where he studied poetry under Lorna Goodison and playwriting under Fred D'Aguiar. He won the Jamaica Cultural Development Commission, Best Adult Poet 2014 and 2017. Latest offering of poems, *The Gathering,* was published in 2017.

Rafel Soler is a Spanish poet, an award-winning novelist and university professor. He has published five books of poetry: *Los sitios interiores* (1979), *Maneras de volver* (2009), *Las cartas que debía* (2011), *Ácido almíbar* (2014, Crítica Valenciana Prize, Spain, 2016) and *No eres nadie hasta que te disparan* (2016). Two of his anthologies have been published in Latin America, and some of his books have been translated into English, French, Italian, Japanese, Hungarian and Romanian.

Mark Spitzer is the author of thirty books. His poetry collections include *GLURK! A Hellbender Odyssey* (2016), *Crypto-Arkansas* (2013), *Age of the Demon Tools* (2008) and book-length translations of Arthur Rimbaud, Jean Genet and Georges Bataille. Spitzer is currently a professor of creative writing at the University of Central Arkansas and the editor-in-chief of Toad Suck Éditions, an Imprint of Mad Hat Press.

K. Srilata is a professor of English at IIT Madras, India. She has five collections of poetry, the latest of which, *The Unmistakable*

Presence of Absent Humans, was published in 2019. Srilata has also written a novel, *Table for Four* (2011) and is co-editor of the anthology *Rapids of a Great River: The Penguin Book of Tamil Poetry* (2009).

Margo Taft Stever's second full-length collection of poetry, *Cracked Piano* and her chapbook, *Ghost Moose* were both published in 2019. Her other poetry collections include *The Lunatic Ball* (2015) and *The Hudson Line* (2012). Her poetry collection, *Frozen Spring*, won the 2002 Mid-List Press First Series Award for Poetry, and *Reading the Night Sky*, won the 1996 Riverstone Poetry Chapbook Competition. She is the founder of The Hudson Valley Writers' Center and the founding and co-editor of Slapering Hol Press.

Toni Giselle Stuart is a South African poet, performer and spoken word educator. Her work is published in anthologies, journals and non-fiction books globally. Her work includes Krotoa-Eva's Suite—a cape jazz poem in three movements—in collaboration with filmmaker Kurt Orderson (2016), I Come To My Body As A Question with dotdotdot dance (2016 - 2020), and forgetting. and memory with vangile gantsho & Vusumzi Ngxande, at the Virtual National Arts Festival (South Africa, 2020).

Terese Svoboda, born in Nebraska, U.S., is an American poet, novelist, memoirist, short story writer, librettist, translator, biographer, critic and videomaker. She has published eight books of poetry. *Theatrix: Play Poems* was published in 2021. A Guggenheim fellow, she has been awarded the Bobst Prize in fiction, the Iowa Prize for poetry, an NEH grant for translation, the Graywolf Nonfiction Prize, a Jerome Foundation prize for video, the O. Henry Award for short story, and a Pushcart Prize for essay. Her opera *WET* premiered at Los Angeles Disney Hall.

George Szirtes was born in Hungary. He emigrated to England with his parents—survivors of concentration and labour camp after the 1956 Budapest uprising. He has won a variety of prizes for his work. His poetry collection, *Reel* (2004) won the T.S. Eliot Prize. He won the Bess Hokin Prize in 2008 for poems published in the *Poetry* magazine. His translations from Hungarian poetry, fiction and drama have also won numerous awards. His latest work is *Mapping the Delta* (2016).

Marianne Szlyk is a professor at Montgomery College, USA, where she is also an assistant poetry editor at *Potomac Review*. She has written books such as *On the Other Side of the Window* (2018) and *Poetry en Plein Air* (2018).

Katherine Barrett Swett lives in New York City. She received a Ph.D. in American Literature from Columbia University. Her poems have been published in various journals including, *The Lyric, Rattle, Mezzo Cammin, The Raintown Review* and *Measure*. Erica Dawson selected Swett's collection, *Voice Message*, (2020) for the 2019 Donald Justice Poetry Prize. Her chapbook, *Twenty-One,* was published in 2016.

Bei Ta is a Chinese poet, critic and translator who serves in the National Museum of Modern Chinese Literature. He has thirty books to his credit including poetry and prose. He has translated the selected poems of Rabindranath Tagore.

Anand Thakore is a poet and Hindustani classical vocalist. *Elephant Bathing* (2012), *Mughal Sequence* (2012) and *Waking in December* (2001) are his three collections of verse. He is the founder of Harbour Line, a publishing collective, and Kshitij, an interactive forum for musicians.

Jeet Thayil is an Indian poet and fiction writer who writes in English. His poetry collections include *These Errors Are Correct* (2022), *Apocalypso* and *English* besides his *Collected Poems* (2015). His novel *Narcopolis* won the DSC Prize and has been followed by three other novels including *The Book of Chocolate Saints*.

Alexei Tsvetkov, born in Stanyslaviv, Ukraine is a Russian poet and essayist. In the late 80s he stopped writing poetry and turned to prose. The unfinished novel *Just a Voice*, an autobiography of a fictitious Roman soldier reflects Tsvetkov's idea of the Roman civilization as one of the summits in the history of humanity. In 2004, after a seventeen-year break, Tsvetkov turned back to poetry. In 2007, he was awarded the Andrei Bely prize for poetry.

A.J. Thomas is an Indian English poet, fiction writer, translator and editor. He was editor of *Indian Literature* till 2010, and later its guest editor for seven years. He is the recipient of Katha Award, AKMG Prize and Vodafone Crossword Award (2007).

Anubhav Tulasi is an Indian poet, literary translator, literary critic, film critic, short-fiction writer, and editor. He has authored and edited more than forty books, out of which seventeen are poetry collections in Assamese.

Annakutty Valiamangalam was associate professor in German literature at Banaras Hindu University and professor of German literature and head of the Department of Foreign Languages, University of Bombay (Mumbai). She writes poems in Malayalam, English and German Languages. She has a book of poems in German, *Im Tempel der Worte* (In the Temple of Words), and her poems in English and Malayalam have appeared in many periodicals. She has three books of poetry translated from Malayalam into German that include selected poems of K. Satchidanandan, ONV Kurup and Sugathakumari.

Pramila Venkateswaran is a poet of Indian descent, now settled in U.S. She was the poet laureate of Suffolk County, Long Island, New York from 2013 to 2015. She is the co-director of Matwaala: South Asian Diaspora Poetry Festival. She is the author of several volumes of poetry, the most recent being *The Singer of Alleppey* (2018). She teaches English and Women's Studies at Nassau Community College, New York. She is a founding member of Women Included, a transnational feminist association.

Veerankutty is one of the finest Indian poets of the middle generation in Malayalam and is concerned with nature and environment. He has many volumes of poetry, including *Nishshabdathayude Republic* (The Republic of Silence) and *Mindapraani* (The Dumb Creature). His poems have appeared in English, Tamil and Arabic and he has won several awards including the Kerala Sahitya Akademi award.

Marc Vincenz is an Anglo-Swiss-American poet, a fiction writer, translator, editor, publisher, designer, multi-genre artist and musician. He has published fourteen books of poetry, including *Becoming the Sound of Bees* (2016), *Leaning into the Infinite* (2015), *The Syndicate of Water and Light* (Station Hill Press, 2018), and *Here Comes the Nightdust* (2018). Vincenz is also a prolific translator and has translated from the German, Romanian and French. He has published ten books of translations, most recently *Unexpected Development* by award-winning Swiss poet and novelist Klaus Merz (2018) and which was a finalist for the 2016 Cliff Becker Book Prize in Translation.

Heidi Williamson is an advisory fellow for the Royal Literary Fund. Her first collection, *Electric Shadow* (2011), was a Poetry Book Society recommendation and shortlisted for the Seamus Heaney Centre Prize. *The Print Museum* won the 2016 East Anglian Book Award for Poetry. Her third collection (2020) *Return by Minor Road* talks about her time living in Dunblane at the time of the Primary School shooting and its aftermath.

Michele Wolf is the author of *Immersion* (2011), *Conversations During Sleep* (1998), and the chapbook *The Keeper of Light* (2015). She has won the Anhinga Prize for Poetry, the Anna Davidson Rosenberg award. She has been a contributing editor for *Poet Lore,* and she teaches at The Writer's Center in Bethesda, Maryland.

Sam Wronoski is a poet temporarily living in Boston, Massachusetts. His poetry has appeared in the journals such as *After the Pause* (which nominated his poem, *The Reviews are in* for Sundress Press' Best of the Net award), *Eunoia Review* and *The Boston Compass*, among others.

Tian Xiang, born in Guangxi Province of China, lives in Nanning city and is the vice-president and director of the poetry committee of Guangxi Provincial Writers' Association. He has published six books of poetry including *Snowman* and *Selected Poems*.

Gong Xuan, who hails from Taicang, Jiangsu in China has six collections of poetry, including *Far or Near, Burning* and *Jiangnan*. He has established the Jiangnan Folk Modern Poetry Museum. He has won honours and awards like the Annual Poet of Poetry Monthly (2012) and Top Ten Poets of Modern Youth (2016).

Anton Yakovlev's chapbook, *Chronos Dines Alone* (2018), won the James Tate Poetry Prize 2018. *The Last Poet of the Village*, his book of translations of selected poems by Sergei Yesenin, was published in 2019.

Yang Yujun, born in Beijing, teaches English in Guangdong. Her first collections *Garden in Winter* and *The Hand on the Mouse is Turning Cold* were published in 1986. She has translated thirty Chinese poets into English and the stories of Alice Munro into Chinese. Her poems have appeared in English, Arabic, Japanese and Spanish.

Andrena Zawinski's poetry has received awards for lyricism, form, spirituality, and social concern, several of them Pushcart Prize nominations. Her latest book is *Landings*; others are *Something About* (it won a PEN Oakland Award) and *Traveling in Reflected Light* (a Kenneth Patchen Prize) along with several chapbooks and work appearing widely online and in print. She is a veteran teacher and activist and runs the San Francisco Bay Area Women's Poetry Salon and is features editor at PoetryMagazine.com

William Zhou (Zhou Se-se) was born in Hunan, China. He is a poet, novelist, painter, publisher and documentary film director with many collections of poems including *Under the Pines, Moss, End of the World* and *Rhinoceros*. His fictional works include *Apple* and *Crows of Zhongguancun*.

Eva Christina Zeller is a German poet. She was born in 1960 in Ulm/Donau in Germany and now lives in Tübingen. In 1988, she joined University of Otago in Dunedin, New Zealand as a lecturer. She teaches creative writing at the University of Tübingen Leibnizkolleg. Zeller's poetry has already been conferred with the prestigious Thaddäus-Troll Award. She published eight books of poetry and has been translated into the Portuguese.